A KNITTER'S TEMPLATE

Easy Steps to Great-Fitting Garments

LAURA MILITZER BRYANT AND BARRY KLEIN

Martingale™
& COMPANY

Mission Statement

We are dedicated to providing quality products and service by working together to inspire creativity and to enrich the lives we touch.

Credits

PRESIDENT • Nancy J. Martin
CEO • Daniel J. Martin
PUBLISHER • Jane Hamada
EDITORIAL DIRECTOR • Mary V. Green
MANAGING EDITOR • Tina Cook
TECHNICAL EDITOR • Ursula Reikes
COPY EDITOR • Liz McGehee
DESIGN DIRECTOR • Stan Green
ILLUSTRATOR • Robin Strobel
TEXT DESIGNER • Trina Stahl
COVER DESIGNER • Stan Green
STUDIO PHOTOGRAPHER • Brent Kane
FASHION PHOTOGRAPHER • Zee Wendell
HAIR and MAKEUP • Casey Gouveia
FASHION STYLIST • Emilie Maslow

A Knitter's Template: Easy Steps to Great-Fitting Garments
© 2003 by Laura Militzer Bryant and Barry Klein

Martingale & Company
20205 144th Avenue NE
Woodinville, WA 98072-8478
www.martingale-pub.com

Printed in China
08 07 06 05 04 03   8 7 6 5 4 3 2 1

Library of Congress Cataloging-in-Publication Data
Bryant, Laura Militzer.
    A knitter's template : easy steps to great-fitting garments /
Laura Bryant and Barry Klein.
        p. cm.
    ISBN 1-56477-453-8
    1. Knitting—Patterns. I. Klein, Barry. II. Title.
TT820 .B872 2002
746.43′20432—dc21   2002151308

Dedication

To knitters everywhere, whose passion for our craft keeps us motivated.

✦ ✦ ✦

Acknowledgments

We would like to thank our customers, the retailers, for their enthusiasm and unwavering support of our endeavors, and for promoting us to their customers, the knitters.

The book could not have been done without the loving hands of our knitters: Peggy, Hersick, Fayla, Edna, Jeanne, Martha, Kay, and Marge. They brought substance to what we only imagined. Thank you for all of your efforts.

The staffs of Trendsetter and Prism kept business running while our attention was occupied with book matters. We thank them for their love and dedication: Myrna, Heidi, Zuni, Maggie, Ellie, Jose, and Nicole at Trendsetters; and Matt, Martha, Kay, Lillie, Trudy, and Diane at Prism. We love you back!

The manufacturers of our yarns are very special people, and we thank them for their creativity.

Our sincere thanks go to:

Fayla, for helping Barry to know no creative boundaries;

Edna, for being Barry's guardian angel;

Martha, for always being there and for completing the Prism picture;

Matt—you are a prince among men for your love, help, and support.

Thank you to our sales agents, who reach out to the world on our behalf.

A special thanks to always "on call" Ursula, our technical editor. We appreciate that you work hard to make everything we envision possible.

Thank you to our families, whose nurturing love and support made us the people we are.

CONTENTS

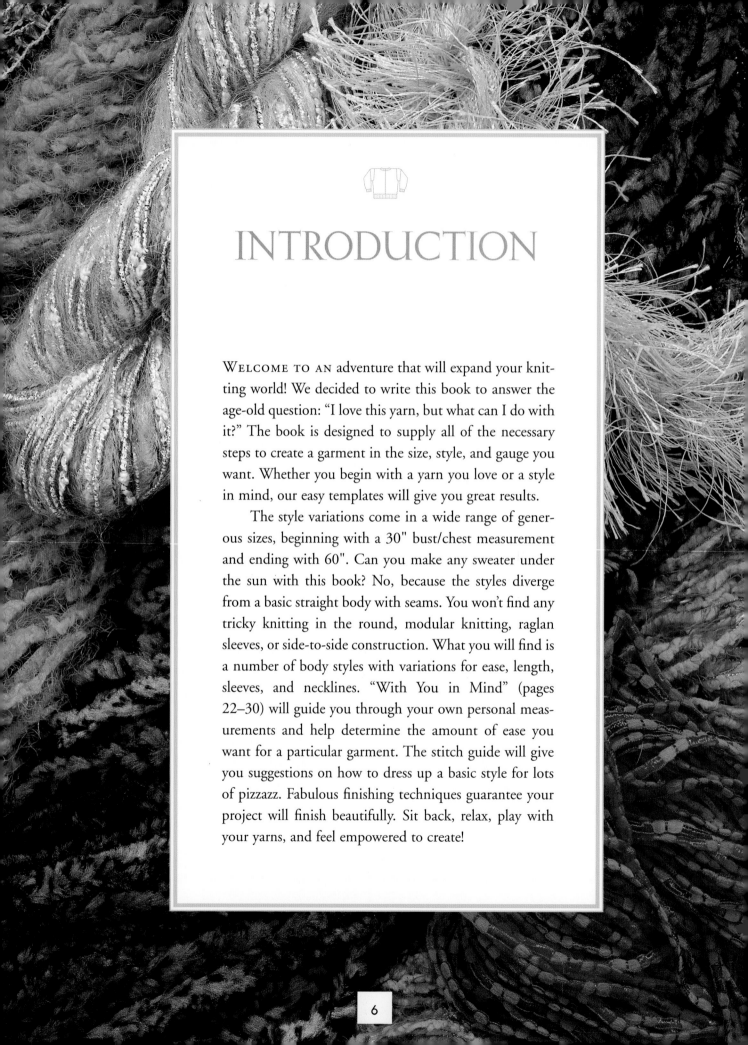

INTRODUCTION

WELCOME TO AN adventure that will expand your knitting world! We decided to write this book to answer the age-old question: "I love this yarn, but what can I do with it?" The book is designed to supply all of the necessary steps to create a garment in the size, style, and gauge you want. Whether you begin with a yarn you love or a style in mind, our easy templates will give you great results.

The style variations come in a wide range of generous sizes, beginning with a 30" bust/chest measurement and ending with 60". Can you make any sweater under the sun with this book? No, because the styles diverge from a basic straight body with seams. You won't find any tricky knitting in the round, modular knitting, raglan sleeves, or side-to-side construction. What you will find is a number of body styles with variations for ease, length, sleeves, and necklines. "With You in Mind" (pages 22–30) will guide you through your own personal measurements and help determine the amount of ease you want for a particular garment. The stitch guide will give you suggestions on how to dress up a basic style for lots of pizzazz. Fabulous finishing techniques guarantee your project will finish beautifully. Sit back, relax, play with your yarns, and feel empowered to create!

USER'S GUIDE
HOW TO MAKE THIS BOOK
WORK FOR YOU

USING THE TEMPLATE is easy! Follow these seven steps for a perfect custom garment:

1. Select a yarn and pattern stitch and determine the gauge (page 8).

2. Select a garment type and then select the styling details (page 8).

3. Select the size based on the amount of ease you wish (page 11).

4. Copy the Blank Pattern Worksheet (page 19) and Style Diagram (page 21).

5. Go to the Measurement Chart (pages 16–17) and find your size. Fill in the Blank Pattern Worksheet with the dimensions for your size and style.

6. Go to the template pages for your stitch gauge and find the column with your size (pages 45–63).

7. Following the column down, enter the numbers for your size onto the Blank Pattern Worksheet at the corresponding letters. Make any allowances for borders, pattern-stitch multiples, and adjustments for a custom fit.

Step 1: Yarn and Gauge

MOST OF us fall in love with a yarn first, then look for an appropriate pattern. Follow the suggestions in "Feelings" (pages 31–34) to determine the correct needle size and gauge for your yarn. How the yarn feels and acts will help determine which style you choose to make. Soft or limp yarns will not work well for tailored jackets; stiff and heavy yarns may not make the best cropped top. Consider also how the garment will be worn and how you want it to sit and move on your body. Think about the intended end use—cotton may not make a great ski sweater, while chunky wool doesn't seem right for a summer top. Sometimes, however, the most interesting fashion breaks the rules—menswear styling with a glitzy yarn, or a big cowl-necked sleeveless pullover in fluffy mohair—so don't hesitate to try something different.

You may wish to use a pattern stitch. If so, now is the time to swatch a variety of stitches to find the one you like. See "Changing the Tone" (pages 35–44) for examples of a number of simple stitch and color-work ideas. Stitch dictionaries provide a wealth of patterns. Make sure the gauge is taken over a 4" swatch, knit in your pattern stitch! If you are using a stitch with a multiple, record the multiple, plus any edge stitches, on your blank pattern worksheet as well.

Step 2: The Styles

THE BASIC template outlined in this book is for garments knit from the bottom up with side seams, and sleeves knit separately. Although there are many alternatives to this construction, we wanted to allow as many variations as possible for sizing, fit, and gauge within the space of this book.

Body Lengths

We have included both straight-up and tapered body styles, with five different length options. The desired length will often be a guide for whether to taper or work the body straight.

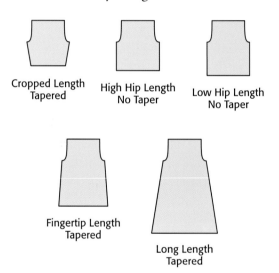

Cropped Length
Tapered

High Hip Length
No Taper

Low Hip Length
No Taper

Fingertip Length
Tapered

Long Length
Tapered

+ *Cropped* tops, which hit just below the waist, are usually tapered from a narrower bottom width to a larger bust measurement. This allows the top to sit properly on the body; if it were knit straight up, the hem would tend to stand out from the body, "flapping in the breeze." This length is usually used for sleeveless or short-sleeved summer tops or dressy evening shells.

+ *High-hip* tops, which hit at the top of the hipbone, are generally knit straight up. The high-hip measurement is usually similar to the bust measurement, so tapering isn't necessary. This length is good for pullovers or sporty cardigans, whether sleeveless, short-sleeved, or long-sleeved. A high-hip length allows a smaller circumference than low-hip or fingertip, since the garment body doesn't need to accommodate hips and ease. This style is more flattering if the hem just grazes the hips.

- *Low-hip* sweaters, which may just cover more of the bottom, must be made with enough ease to accommodate the hips, tapering from a wider hem to a narrower bust. Tapering in this case allows for more ease over the hip, but removes some of the fabric—and thus bulk—before the armhole shaping to allow for a neater shoulder area. Traditional cardigans and oversized pullovers—jackets meant to be worn over slim pants or skirts and most men's garments—are made in this length.

- *Fingertip* garments reach to the fingers when the arm is relaxed and the fingers slightly curled. Car coats, long tunics, and jackets are worked to this length, which will taper from a wider hem to a narrower bust, or will be large enough to provide ease in the hips. Tapered knitting of this length often hangs better than straight.

- *Long* knitted coats or vests can be extremely dramatic. This length will often have taper built in, or it will be sized large enough to provide ease in the hips if made with straight shaping. Even more ease should be allowed for, since longer knitting tends to get heavy, and as it does, it grows even longer and becomes narrower. A long length should be carefully adjusted for the wearer and should include a period of hanging the piece to allow for natural stretch before finishing the armhole and shoulder shaping.

NOTE: Taper in cropped sweaters that begin with a narrower hem and increase to the bust measurement is almost always worked at the side seams only. Taper from a wider hem to a narrower bust can either be worked at the side seams or divided between the side seams and two marked "darts," located roughly one-third of the width from each side edge. To achieve more taper on a shorter garment, use the cast-on numbers for a long coat and decrease more often to get to the bust measurement. If the decreases are spread across the four points, you avoid making a triangle whose side edges (seams) are longer than the middle, and the garment will hang better at the hem. This is necessary only if decreasing more than two or three inches from the total width.

Body and Neckline Styles

- *Pullovers* are exactly that: there is no front opening, and the garments are "pulled over" the head. Pullover neck shaping includes a shallow V neck, three different rounded shapes, and a boat neck. The rounded shapes are scoop, which is low and appropriate for tank-top styles; crew neck, which is high and the basis for building traditional ribbed neckbands, turtlenecks, and mock necks; and jewel, which is in between and usually finished simply. Boat necks are straight across with no shaping and are wider than shaped necklines. Funnel necks are built onto boat-neck shaping.

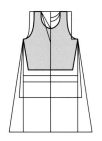
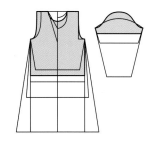

Cropped Length with Taper
Sleeveless Cut-In Armhole
Scoop Neck

High Hip No Taper
Set-In Cap Sleeve
Jewel Neck

✦ *Classic cardigans* are pullovers split up the middle, with an overlapping button band, and are often worked with no taper. Deep V, shallow V, and crew necklines all work well for classic cardigans. Shawl collars are built upon deep V necks, and turned collars are built upon crew shaping. Ribbed, garter, or crocheted bands can finish any of the three.

Fingertip Jacket with Taper
Shallow V Neck
Modified Drop Long Sleeve

✦ *Tailored jackets* are also pullovers split up the middle, but they have a center front that just meets, and so are appropriate for dressier styles with no button, button and loop, or zipper closure. Deep V, shallow V, or crew necklines work here. Edges such as applied I-cord (page 141) are a good choice for finishing, as is crochet with reverse single crochet (page 142). Because there may not be a closure, more ease should be allowed so the jacket doesn't gap in the front, or tapering should be used.

Tailored Jacket No Taper
Set-In Cap Sleeve
Crew Neck

✦ *Coats* are oversized cardigans: longer, with taper built in or generous in circumference if straight. There is overlap allowed for the front closure, and extra ease should be considered to accommodate other garments underneath and also for the narrowing that occurs from the weight of the knitting. Deep V, shallow V, and crew necklines work well with this style.

Long Coat with Taper
Modified Drop Long Sleeve
Deep V Neck

Sleeve and Armhole Styles

✦ Sleeveless styles can have either standard or cut-in armholes. Standard armholes will hit the shoulders just inside where the arm joins the shoulder, and they allow for a bit more coverage. Cut-in armholes are another inch or so inside of the shoulder line.

✦ Cap, short, and long sleeves can be attached to either standard set-in armhole shaping, where the armhole is rounded and the top of the sleeve has a true cap, or to a modified drop shaping, where the armhole cuts in sharply once and then knits straight up. The modified drop sleeve has a gently rounded cap, and the shoulder line is extended beyond the natural shoulder of the body.

Set-In Armhole Shaping
True Cap Sleeve

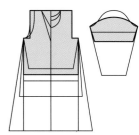

Modified Drop Sleeve
Gently Rounded Cap Sleeve

Step 3: What Size Am I?

THE CHAPTER "With You in Mind" takes you step by step through custom measurements. No true universal sizing exists: Laura, who at 5'3" has broad shoulders, a short torso, and an athletic build, wears sizes that range from an 8 to a 12 in ready-to-wear and uses a size 14 sewing pattern. She makes a finished bust that ranges anywhere from 38" for a dressy sweater or summer top to 44" for a coat or jacket. This lack of continuity is why we decided to eliminate size designations and use only inch measurements to distinguish one size from another. So, from this day forth, you are no longer a size!

It is important to know all of the nuances of your own shape for truly great-fitting garments, so take the time to fill in the measurement chart. Once you have selected the garment style and yarn, the next step is to determine the amount of ease you desire. Consider the following:

✦ Is the garment short or long? The longer the garment, the more ease required.

✦ Is the garment a pullover or cardigan? Cardigans need to have enough ease to allow for garments worn under them; pullovers may be more fitted if dressier, or larger if more sporty or if a turtleneck will be worn underneath.

Cardigans require more ease than pullovers.

A shorter garment requires little ease;
a longer garment requires more.

11

What is the yarn like—thick or thin, soft or stiff? Thick or stiff yarns should have enough ease for comfort of wear, but not so much that they take on a size of their own and make one seem larger. Soft or thin yarns can either be fitted or have a lot of ease for a draped look. Look at ready-to-wear: loose and flowing garments are made of very thin, soft material, while thicker wools tend to be tailored for a close fit.

Firm Yarn, Drapable Ribbon, and
Soft and Lofty Mohair

Is there a large difference between your bust and hip? Be sure to make the size that accommodates the larger measurement, and if the difference is substantial (more than 4"), consider adding taper in either direction, regardless of the style.

Taper can be added to accommodate a significant
measurement difference between bust and hip.

Are your shoulders square or sloped? If square, you may choose to finish your shoulders straight across in one bind-off. If sloped, select the shaped shoulder option (page 29).

Sloping the shoulders gives a more fitted look.

Notice that our charts do not refer to a size as "small," "medium," or "large," but simply as a finished bust/chest measurement. Select the size you will make from the desired finished measurement of the garment, once you have taken into account all of the preceding factors.

Customize your size by referring to the measurements taken in the chapter on fit. The most crucial difference between people's sizes, and the most important fitting point, is the shoulder-width measurement. Everything about the way a garment fits flows from how it sits on the shoulders. Thin people can have broad shoulders; large people can have narrow shoulders. Our sizes have been written progressively larger: as the girth increases, so do the length, shoulder width, and armhole depth.

The increases are proportional, but notice that although the girth numbers change dramatically, measurements such as shoulders change far less. So, if you are making a large size, there will be much more decreasing for armhole shaping to get to an appropriate shoulder size than if you were making a small size. Likewise, if you are making a small size, there may be very little shaping. If your shoulder measurement differs from the selected size, which it may easily do, find the right shoulder measurement from the "Measurement Chart" on pages 16–17. Find the column for this size on the gauge page and locate the armhole shaping. The number of stitches that are left after doing all armhole decreases is the number you want for your garment, so decrease more or fewer stitches as needed to get to this number. Also check the armhole depth and make note of any change you wish there. If the armhole depth changes, the sleeve width at the top (for a modified drop) or the cap depth (for a set-in sleeve) will also change. For any change you need to make, locate the correct measurement on the size chart and then refer to the stitch numbers on the gauge pages for that size.

From large to small—the templates cover it all!

Steps 4–7: Pattern Writing

Turn to the "Measurement Chart" on pages 16–17 and find the column for your finished size. Copy the measurements onto the style diagram (page 21) so you have a ready reference as you knit.

Your blank pattern worksheet should already have the gauge and needle size entered at the top. Turn to the pages for your gauge and select the column with your finished bust/chest measurement. Following the instructions at the left side for the body style you have selected, enter the numbers from the column for your size onto the blank pattern. The blank spaces and the size charts are labeled with letters that correspond to the numbers you need to find.

If you are adding a pattern stitch, adjust the pattern numbers as follows:

1. Subtract the number of edge stitches from the cast-on total. The repeat of a pattern stitch is written as "multiple of ___ plus ___." The edge stitches are the "plus" number.

2. Divide the remaining stitches by the multiple. If the divisor is even, you are all set. If it is a fraction, you need to round up or down to make it even. Round up if you wish a bit more ease (or if the fraction is over .5). Round down if there is plenty of ease (or if the fraction is under 5).

    For example: Suggested cast-on for a 40" circumference (a 20" back) is 90 stitches for a gauge of 4.5 sts = 1". The pattern repeat is 6 plus 3. Subtract 3 from 90 = 87. Divide 87 by 6 = 14.5 repeats. Round up to 15 repeats times 6 = 90 stitches plus 3 = 93 stitches cast on.

There are several things you can tweak for perfect results. We did not allow for selvage stitches. If your garment is close fitting, add two stitches to every piece for seaming. The rate of increases and decreases for taper and V-neck shaping are based on the stated body length with set-in armhole shaping. Cut-in (sleeveless) and modified-drop armholes change the length of the garment to the armhole by a small amount, but the rates of increase and decrease will hold true. If your row gauge is different from the stated row gauge, find a row gauge that matches yours from a different chart. Take the stitch numbers from the matching stitch gauge, but find a column (regardless of the size) whose number of increases or decreases is the same as yours in the chart with the matching row gauge. Whatever the rate of change is in that column, use that number (decrease one stitch each edge every ___ row) as your rate.

The cast-on numbers are written for a borderless finish (no ribbing). Many styles begin with simple rows of garter stitch (which require no change in numbers) or are in fabric flat enough that a crocheted edge is all that is necessary. A good rule of thumb for any rib or garter stitch on a border is to use a needle two sizes smaller than the body. Additionally, rib stitches should be about 10 percent fewer in number than the body stitches. Make notes of any changes between the border stitches and body/sleeve stitches.

Contrary to our early knitting teaching, row gauge is not something to be ignored, but a helpful tool both in ensuring good results and in planning quantities of yarn. If your row gauge varies much from the stated gauge on a pattern, you will use more yarn (if you knit more rows per inch) or less yarn (if you knit fewer rows per inch) than the pattern calls for. We have found over the years that variations in row gauge are the biggest differences from one knitter to another. Needle sizes can be changed to match a stitch gauge—but the row gauge still might not match. Not to worry; most of the time this only impacts amount of yarn, because knitting that is worked from the bottom is knit to a measurement. Novelty yarns in particular,

because they are heavy, tend to have fewer rows per inch. Many pattern stitches, especially those with slipped stitches, have more rows per inch. Be aware of differences, and make adjustments as needed.

Ribbed and cabled stitches require some extra planning. Because these stitches tend to pull in, the ratio of stitches to rows changes, with more stitches in relation to rows per inch. This mostly affects sleeve cap and shoulder shaping, where the extra stitches will result in cap shaping that occurs too slowly, leaving a large number of stitches at the top or a too-wide shoulder seam. The answer is to increase the rate of cap decreases; for example, "Arroyo Avenue" (page 89) has decreases that occur every row instead of every other row. When binding off at the top edge, decrease the stitches as you bind off by working two stitches together as many times as necessary to return to a normal number of stitches (compare the gauge of the yarn in stockinette to the gauge in pattern—the stockinette numbers are the more normal gauge). A rib pattern with more knits than purls will not need as many decreases as a regular rib. Cables can be decreased in the middle of the cable, usually by two stitches.

Two ribbed swatches: one relaxed, one slightly stretched; take care when measuring your gauge.

The Fudge Factor

EVERY DESIGNER employs a fudge factor, and we are no exception. Our size proportions and incremental changes are based on our joint years of designing, teaching, measuring, and "fixing." When writing different sizes and calculating numbers of stitches, fractions invariably show up. In almost every instance, we rounded up, unless the fraction was ¼" or less.

Additionally, the finer the gauge, the more precise the shaping can be; conversely, larger gauges require more fudging. In the smaller gauges, you will find that there are distinct differences between sizes; as the gauges get larger, the numbers will tend to stay the same for several sizes and then change.

How Much Yarn Do I Want?

OF COURSE, we all want as much yarn as we can afford! However, since few of us have unlimited yarn budgets, we want a realistic idea of how much yarn to buy for a given garment. This is one of the toughest areas to address, since so many factors influence the final yarn requirement. The "Yardage Chart" on page 18 shows suggested yardages for each range of gauges, in each range of sizes. We have organized it this way to give you guidance, but there is no ultimate answer. You will find that the yarn requirements for the patterns in this book all fall within the ranges on the charts. Important questions to ask when deciding on quantities:

+ Am I a tight or loose knitter? Generally, even when knitting a stitch gauge, a loose knitter will knit a looser row gauge (that is, fewer rows per inch) than a tight knitter (more rows per inch). Tighter knitters will need more yardage.

+ Is my garment on the smaller or larger side of the size range? Obviously, slightly smaller garments will require less yardage; larger sizes, more.

+ Is the gauge on the smaller or larger side? In this case, the smaller gauge needs more yardage (more stitches and rows per inch, thus more yardage needed); the larger gauges, less.

+ Is there a pattern stitch? Pattern knitting usually uses about 25 percent more yarn. This is especially true when more than one color is used. The extra goes to carrying yarn along the back and to the remnants of skeins left when all knitting is complete. Cables and other stitches that pull in can be compensated for by using the chart for the smaller gauge range (taken over the cables or rib), but remember that although the stitch gauge got smaller, the row gauge did not and you can compromise between the yardage requirements.

Whatever you calculate your needs to be, buy an extra skein. When the first piece is completed, check to see how much yarn has been used. Hopefully you are on target, but if you think you might be close, now is the time to get another skein, before the yarn/color/dye lot is changed or discontinued. As much as we value our hard-earned dollars, the real heartbreak is in investing a lot of money and time into a project that cannot be finished! Any extra yarn can go into your stash for use with other yarns later and can be invaluable if you need to repair something in the future.

Measurement Chart (All measurements are in inches.)

Finished Bust/Chest	30	32	34	36	38	40
Body Length (D+I)						
Cropped	18	18	18½	18½	19	19
High Hip	20	20	20½	20½	21	21
Low Hip	22	22	22½	22½	23	23
Fingertip	26	26	27	27	28	28
Long	38	38	39	39	40	40
Armhole Depth (I)						
Sleeveless	6½	6½	6½	7	7	7
Set In	7	7	7	7½	7½	7½
Modified Drop	7½	7½	7½	8	8	8
Neckline (from beg of armhole)						
Crew	4½	4½	4½	5	5	5
Jewel	3½	3½	3½	4	4	4
Scoop or Shallow V	2½	2½	2½	2	2	2
Deep V	-1	-1	-1	-1	-1	-1
Shoulder Width						
Cut In	11	11	11½	11½	11½	12
Set In	12½	13	13½	13½	14	14
Modified Drop	14	14	15	15	16	16
Back Neck Width						
Boat Neck	8	8	8	8	9	9
All Others	5	5	5½	5½	6	6
Sleeve Length						
Set In						
Cap (to ua)	1½	1½	1½	1½	2	2
Cap (total L)	5½	5½	5½	6	6½	6½
Short Sleeve (to ua)	4	4	4	4	4½	4½
Short Sleeve (total L)	8	8	8	8½	9	9
Long Sleeve (to ua)	15	15	15½	15½	16	16
Long Sleeve (total L)	19	19	19½	20	20½	20½
Modified Drop						
Cap (total L)*	4½	4½	4½	5	5½	5½
Short Sleeve (total L)*	7	7	7	7½	8	8
Long Sleeve (total L)*	18	18	18½	19	19½	19½

Measurement to underarm for cap, short, and long modified drop sleeve is total length minus 3".

ua = underarm; L = length

42	44	46	48	50	52	54	56	58	60
19	19½	19½	20	20	20	20½	20½	21	21
21	21½	21½	22	22	22	22½	22½	23	23
23	23½	23½	24	24	24	24½	24½	25	25
28	29	29	30	30	30	31	31	32	32
40	41	41	42	43	43	44	45	45	46
7½	7½	7½	8	8	8	8½	8½	8½	8½
8	8	8	8½	8½	8½	9	9	9½	9½
8½	8½	8½	9	9	9	9½	9½	10	10
5½	5½	5½	6	6	6	6½	6½	7	7
4½	4½	4½	5	5	5	5½	5½	6	6
2½	2½	2½	3	3	3	3½	3½	3½	3½
-1	-1	-1	-1	-1	-1	-1	-1	-1	-1
12	12	12½	12½	13	13	13½	13½	14	14
14½	15	15½	16	16½	17	17½	17½	18	18
17	17	18	19	20	20	21	21	22	22
9	9	9	9	10	10	10	10	10	10
6	6½	6½	6½	7	7	7	7	7	7
2	2	2	2½	2½	2½	2½	3	3	3
7	7	7	8	8	8	8½	9	9½	9½
4½	4½	4½	5	5	5	5	5½	5½	5½
9½	9½	9½	10	10	10	10½	11	11½	11½
16	16½	16½	16½	17	17	17	17½	17½	18
21	21½	21½	22	22½	22½	23	23½	24	24½
6	6	6	6½	6½	6½	7	7½	7½	7½
8½	8½	8½	8½	8½	8½	9	9½	9½	9½
20	20½	20½	20½	21	21	21½	22	22	22½

17

YARDAGE CHART

THE FOLLOWING chart indicates approximate total yards of yarn required for the various styles and sizes. Use these amounts as guidelines only. Actual amounts will vary depending on type of yarn, pattern stitch, and individual differences in tension of knitting.

Style/Sizes	6sts = 1"	5–5.5sts = 1"	4–4.5sts = 1"	3–3.5sts = 1"	2–2.5sts = 1"
Sleeveless	Yards	Yards	Yards	Yards	Yards
30–36	600–700	500–700	450–600	350–450	200–300
38–44	850–1000	750–950	650–850	500–650	300–400
46–52	1000–1150	1050–1250	900–1050	700–850	500–600
54–60	1200–1350	1300–1450	1100–1250	900–1000	600–700
Short Sleeves					
30–36	1000–1150	950–1050	800–900	750–850	350–450
38–44	1200–1350	1150–1350	1000–1150	875–1000	450–550
46–52	1400–1550	1350–1500	1200–1350	1000–1125	550–650
54–60	1600–1800	1550–1700	1400–1600	1150–1300	650–750
Long Sleeves					
30–36	1300–1600	1050–1300	900–1200	600–900	600–700
38–44	1750–2100	1350–1600	1300–1600	950–1200	700–800
46–52	2300–2500	1650–1800	1650–1950	1250–1500	850–1000
54–60	2650–2800	1850–2200	2000–2200	1550–1700	1050–1200
Fingertip Jacket					
30–36	1600–1750	1450–1550	1250–1350	900–1100	700–800
38–44	1800–1950	1600–1750	1450–1550	1150–1350	800–900
46–52	2000–2150	1800–1950	1600–1750	1400–1550	900–1000
54–60	2200–2350	2000–2150	1800–1950	1600–1750	1000–1100
Long Coat					
30–36	2100–2800	1850–2650	1600–2300	1200–1700	900–1000
38–44	3000–3500	2800–3350	2450–2850	1750–2100	1000–1100
46–52	3600–4050	3500–3950	2950–3350	2150–2500	1150–1250
54–60	4100–4500	4000–4250	3400–3600	2550–2700	1300–1400

Blank Pattern Worksheet

Style: _____

    Length: _____

    Optional taper: _____

    Sleeves

        Length: _____

        Armhole style: _____

    Neckline style: _____

Size: _____

Materials: _____

Needles: _____

Stitch Pattern (name): _____ and (multiple) _____

Gauge: _____ sts and _____ rows = 1" (measured over 4" swatch)

BACK

With size _____ needle, CO _____ sts (A, plus or minus any adjustments for border). Work desired border for _____".

Change needles, if necessary, and inc or dec _____ sts across next row. Total sts: _____ (A) (the number from the charts for your size).

Optional taper (cropped): Inc 1 st at each end every _____ rows _____ times (B). Total sts = _____ .

Optional taper (fingertip or long): Dec 1 st at each end every _____" _____ times (C). Total sts = _____ .

Work to _____" (D) (from diagram).

SHAPE ARMHOLE

Cut-in or set-in: BO _____ sts at beg of next _____ rows (E). Dec 1 st at each end EOR _____ times (F). Dec 1 st at each end every 4th row _____ times (G). Total sts = _____ .

Modified drop: BO _____ sts at beg of next 2 rows (H).

Work even to armhole depth of _____" (I) (from diagram). **Total length of garment _____" (I + D)** (from diagram).

OPTIONAL SHOULDER SHAPING

BO _____ sts at beg of next _____ rows (determine this by following instructions on page 29) or BO all sts.

FRONT (PULLOVER)

Work as for back to _____" (desired length for chosen neck style—see size charts). Cont to work armhole shaping as for back, and at the same time…

SHAPE NECK

Boat neck: BO center _____ sts (J).

Any rounded style: BO center _____ sts (K). Attach yarn to 2nd shoulder, and working both shoulders at once, BO _____ sts (L) at each neck edge once; BO _____ sts (M) at each neck edge once, dec 1 st at each neck edge EOR _____ times (N).

Any V style: Work to within 2 sts of center, dec 1 st, attach 2nd ball of yarn and dec 1 st (division for V neck made), cont to dec 1 st at each neck edge every _____ row _____ times (O).

When same length as back, shape shoulders as for back.

FRONT (CARDIGAN OR JACKET)

Cast on _____ sts (P). Work border as for back, then change needles, if necessary, and inc or dec sts evenly across next row. (Determine as for back.)

Optional taper (fingertip or long): Dec 1 st at side edge only every _____ rows _____ times (Q).

Work to _____" (desired length to armhole shaping—see size charts and personal data).

Shape armhole as for back at side edge only. Work to desired length for chosen neck style (see size charts).

SHAPE NECK

Any rounded style: BO _____ sts (R) at neck edge only, BO _____ sts once (L), BO _____ sts once (M), dec 1 st at neck edge only EOR _____ times (N).

Boat neck: BO _____ sts at neck edge only (J).

Any V neck: Dec 1 st at neck edge every _____ rows _____ times (O).

Shape shoulders as for back.

SLEEVES

With size _____ needle, CO _____ sts (S). Work desired border, then change needle, if necessary, and inc or dec _____ sts across next row (depending on border—see back). Beg inc 1 st at each edge every _____ rows _____ times (T). When sleeve is desired length to underarm (see size charts and personal data), shape cap.

SHAPE CAP

Set-in: BO _____ sts (U) at beg of next 2 rows, dec 1 st at each edge EOR to cap depth of _____" (V). BO all sts.

Modified drop: BO _____ sts at beg of next _____ rows (W). BO all sts.

FINISHING

NOTES:

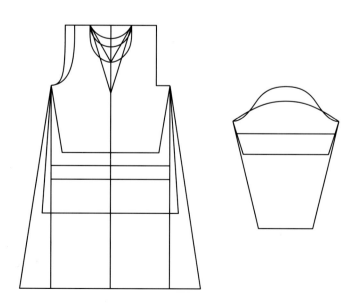

Style Diagram

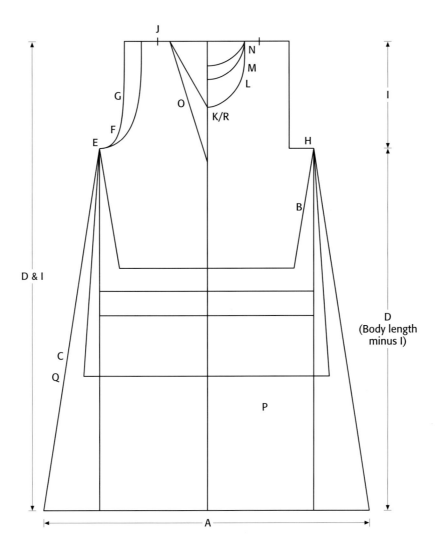

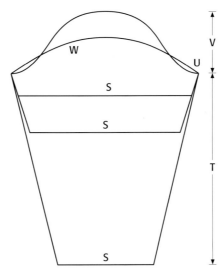

WITH YOU IN MIND
CUSTOM FITTING
TECHNIQUES

BEFORE STARTING YOUR next knitting project, ask yourself: Do I know the size I need to make for the finished sweater to fit the way I want? This section takes you through the process of answering this question in detail. Our goal is to help you feel more comfortable about selecting the right size for yourself or the lucky recipient of your talents.

Body Measurements

WHEN WE teach classes on fit and style, everyone cringes when we talk about taking body measurements. Then, when we get down to it, laughter takes over and the reality is that we learn more about ourselves and what we need to have a sweater that truly fits. Grab a tape measure (a new, nonretractable one is preferable) and a friend. Make a photocopy of the blank "Actual Body Measurement Chart" on page 25 and you're ready to start.

Accurate body measurements are important for deciding which size you will follow in a preprinted knitting pattern and which numbers to use when custom designing your own. You'll learn how to take fitted body measurements and how much ease to add for the different design styles. Then you can find the proper size on the appropriate gauge template.

Working with a friend is a good idea, since taking your own measurements is not easy. If you do decide to work alone, please do so in front of a mirror. This will ensure that the area you are measuring is correct and that the tape measure is in the right place and is completely straight. If you work with a friend, measure your friend and let your friend measure you. Follow the "Actual Body Measurement Chart" as you go. The process of measuring is the same for a woman, man, or child. An alternative to measuring the body is to measure a finished sweater. While this is not as accurate, it will work if you take the same measurements and fill in the chart. If you do measure a finished sweater, note on the chart that these measurements are not "fit" measurements, but finished measurements, including ease.

1. **Bust/Chest:** Work with the tape measure completely straight around the fullest part of the bust/chest. Be sure that the tape fits, but is not digging in, and follows an even horizontal line around the body.

2. **Waist:** Work with the tape measure completely straight around the narrowest part of the body between the bust and the hip. This is usually just inside the waistband of pants or a skirt. Again, the tape should fit but not dig in. You may not have a waist that is narrower than bust or hip, but this measurement is still useful and will help ensure that an accurate size is knit for longer pullovers, jackets, or coats and for cropped, tapered tops.

3. **Hip/Bottom:** The tape should be wrapped around the fullest part of the hip and bottom. It is important to be honest about where you are measuring, since some of us have generous tummies, some of us have prominent bottoms, and some have both. Be sure to write down the number from the larger of the two. When making a coat of any style or a longer classic cardigan, this measurement will make a difference in taper, fit, and ease.

4. **Sleeve Length:** Measure from the top of the shoulder down to the desired length for a short sleeve (A), and down to the wrist, running the tape measure along the arm, for a long sleeve (B). Your wrist is just above the wrist bone when your hand is held up. Note that this measurement is for total length and includes both sleeve length to underarm and sleeve cap.

5. **Back Neck Width:** This is never easy to take and is truly a visual measurement. I usually have the person I am measuring stand facing me. I hold the tape behind their head and measure in a straight line from ear to ear. The back neck controls the opening for the head to fit through. If too much is left open, the sleeves and body do not stay up, and if the opening is too small, the head will not fit through.

6. **Finished Length:** This measurement starts at the bone at the base of the back of the neck with the tape measure going straight down.

A is the length for cropped tops, B is the length for high-hip pullovers/jackets, C is the length for low hip, D is the length for fingertip, and E is the length for coats. Be sure that, for each measurement, you are standing straight up and not leaning in any direction, because this will change the length measured.

7. **Upper Arm:** For some reason, we get the loudest groans when we measure this in a class setting. The tape measure should be wrapped around the fullest part of the upper arm. Be sure that the tape is straight and that it is not digging in. Since most people make short sleeves to cover this area, we will then have the upper arm measurement for a short-sleeve cuff.

8. **Wrist:** Now we get to everyone's favorite measurement. The groans stop here. Measure in a straight line around the wrist just above the wrist bone when your hand is held up.

9. **Shoulders:** This is one of the most important measurements for sleeveless sweaters and for styles with set-in sleeves. A correct measurement will put the sleeve cap at the top of the shoulder for set-in sleeves and will cover up bra straps for sleeveless tops. With the person you are measuring facing away from you, place the tape measure along the inside of the skin fold where the arm attaches to the body and measure horizontally across the shoulder blades to the same point on the other side. Hold the tape and look straight up to see if this is the correct place. Ask yourself: Will the bra straps be covered? Will sleeve caps sit at the top of the shoulder if the sleeve is attached at this point? Adjust the tape in or out, depending on how you answer the questions and in relation to what you want to cover up or show.

10. **Armhole Depth:** Place a knitting needle horizontally under your armpit so that the ends stick out at the front and back. Measure from the needle up along the body to the top of the shoulder.

11. **V Depth:** Put the tape measure at the edge of the neckline, at the center of the shoulder where the seam would be, and run it straight down to your desired depth for a pullover (A) and for a cardigan (B).

12. **Rounded Neck Depth:** Put the tape measure at the edge of the neckline, at the center of the shoulder as for the V, and run it straight down to your desired depth for a crew neck (A), jewel neck (B), or scoop neck (C).

Now that you have taken the measurements, sit down and relax. No matter what the numbers say, it is important to know that no one will see them when you are wearing the perfect-fitting sweater. What will be admired is how beautiful you look and how the sweater accentuates the parts of your body that you want to show off. Remember, we don't wear our size labels on the outside.

ACTUAL BODY MEASUREMENT CHART

For: _____ 		Date: _____

1. Bust/Chest: _____

2. Waist: _____

3. Hip/Bottom: _____

4. Sleeve Length

    A. Short sleeve: _____

    B. Long sleeve: _____

5. Back Neck Width: _____

6. Finished Length

    A. Cropped: _____

    B. High hip: _____

    C. Low hip: _____

    D. Fingertip: _____

    E. Coat: _____

7. Upper Arm: _____

8. Wrist: _____

9. Shoulders: _____

10. Armhole: _____

11. V Depth

    A. Pullover: _____

    B. Cardigan: _____

12. Rounded Neck Depth

    A. Crew: _____

    B. Jewel: _____

    C. Scoop: _____

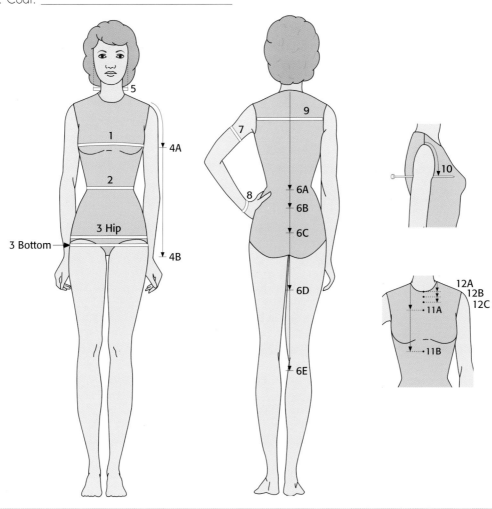

Style Options

LET'S MOVE on to each of the styles that are featured in the projects (pages 64–135) and how to apply your measurements to them. As we look at the different shapes, keep in mind the way you like things to fit. Always remember that we took "fitted" body measurements. You need to decide how much ease you want to add to the different styles. We make our recommendations, but the final decision is up to you.

Shell

This style is made to be worn under a suit jacket or on its own as a top. Most of the time a shell is sleeveless and more form fitting. Armhole shaping is very important and is often worked in full-fashion decreases so that the shaping becomes a part of the design. (A full-fashion decrease is a decorative detail done by placing decreases one or two stitches from the edges.) Armhole shaping also continues higher and at a slower rate for the best fit and most body coverage. Accurate shoulder measurements are very important here. The length of most shells is cropped or high hip so it will not peek out from the bottom of a suit jacket. If the shell is to be worn alone, the length can be made longer with a straighter shaping. We recommend adding either no ease or ease up to 2" to the largest measurement.

Short-Sleeve Top

This style is similar to the shell but with a short sleeve of varying length, usually about 5" to the underarm. Some people like a modified short sleeve, or cap sleeve, with a sleeve length of 1" to 2". Armholes here come a bit lower, allowing for more ease because a short-sleeve top is rarely made to be worn under anything else. The body style is also easier, with less shaping, and you can decide the ultimate length you want. When deciding on a size, think about your bust/chest measurement and add some ease. We consider the addition of about 2" appropriate, depending on how you like your sweaters to fit and how thick the yarn is.

Long-Sleeve Pullover

Laura describes this style as the perfect blank canvas on which to create, similar to the short-sleeved top but with a long sleeve. Our sweaters show how you can go wild. The body can be fitted with shaping, or you can add extra inches to the biggest body measurement and go long. For those with full figures, we often add 4" of ease to the largest measurement, go long in length, and leave a side-vent opening, allowing the sweater to move with the wearer.

Classic Cardigan

Best described as "the sweater you always reach for" or "my favorite old friend," classic cardigans keep us warm and happy. Lengths vary from high hip to low hip and sometimes even longer. The length you select will guide the amount of ease needed. Compare the bust/chest measurement and the hip/bottom measurement. If you are making a true classic cardigan, it will have a straight body and enough ease so it doesn't hug against the larger of your body measurements. We usually add 4" or more of ease to the larger measurement, always keeping in mind the stitch and yarn selection. Since this style is often casual, a modified-drop shoulder is a good choice, making the exact shoulder measurement less important and allowing for a fit with more ease. No matter what you do, this style will remain faithful to you over the years.

Tailored Jacket

Popularized by the House of Chanel, these elegant jackets mean business and will take you from casual to dressy. Straight in shape or with very subtle shaping, these jackets sit at high or low hip when worn. This style is often buttonless, so a blouse or knit shell can be worn underneath. Center fronts meet and don't overlap, so add enough ease to the bust measurement so the fronts don't gap.

Coat

This is where you can go crazy. Because coats are long and truly oversized, the options for textures, stitches, and needle-size variations are at your discretion. The important measurements here are the shoulder, bust/chest, and hip/bottom. Most coats are A-line tapered to provide plenty of ease at the hip while staying narrower at the shoulder, or vertical and full for proper fit around the body, with at least 4" added to the hip measurement. If the yarns selected are thick, you may wish to add extra ease. A modified-drop armhole is best because it allows you to wear clothing of any thickness underneath. This is a decorator's dream—have fun.

Other Factors to Consider

SINCE EACH of us was created differently and our desires for fit range from "painted on" to "big and baggy," here are some things to think about before deciding which size to follow on the templates.

✦ *Where will I wear this sweater?* Dressy sweaters are often more fitted, and casual sweaters more generous. Add more or less ease to your fitted body measurements to suit the end use.

✦ *What kind of yarn am I using and how will it hold up?* Play with your yarn(s) while making your stitch gauge. Try different needle sizes to get the suggested gauge. If you are starting from scratch and working from our templates, work with different needles until you appreciate the feel of the yarn and your stitch pattern shows. Hang up your swatch for a day and see if it grows. Wash your swatch carefully and see how the yarn reacts.

✦ *What is my body style?* Am I full-busted with a slender lower body, am I full-bodied all over, or some other combination? You've taken your actual body measurements and now you have to deal with your body on paper. Since you are no longer using sizes but measurement numbers, forget labels and make something that will actually fit. Stand in front of the mirror and look at how you like to wear your sweaters. Do you like things to fit tightly? If yes, add from 0" to 2" to your fit bust measurement. If no, add anywhere from 2" to 4". If your hips are bigger than your bust or if you have a tummy or bottom that sticks out, be sure to look carefully at your actual body measurements. Work a size that tapers to cover the fullness, or work a size that is large enough to go over the fullness and won't pull or stretch.

✦ *How do I like my sleeves?* Some of us want to show off our arms and some of us want to cover up excess flesh. Some of us have "hot flashes," and covering up our arms adds heat to an already hot furnace. No matter what you decide, look at your actual body measurements and compare them to our measurement charts. If necessary, make a sleeve for a different size and adjust the shaping for the cap. Consider the type of sweater you want to make. Dressy sweaters call for set-in sleeves, while casual, easy sweaters work well with a modified-drop style. In some cases, we have worked square armhole shaping, which is the same as for a modified drop, but there is no cap shaping on the sleeve. Do this when you have wide stripes on a sleeve or a complicated stitch pattern that will cause problems with multiple-row bind-offs along the cap. The sleeve needs to be wide enough to fit into the armhole. Then, just bind off all stitches evenly across your last row.

✦ *How much neck do I like to show?* You've got that million-dollar necklace and you just have to show it off. You're knitting a sweater for that ski trip in Aspen. Both circumstances sound great and each one calls for a different style of neckline. Our template offers you many different variations. Also think about the type of collar finishing you want. For a simple crochet, bring your neck shaping up higher. If you want borders, edges, or collars, bring your shaping down a bit to allow for the extra knitting that will be done.

✦ *Do I need to do shoulder shaping?* Look in the mirror at the slope or angle of your shoulders. If your shoulders are relatively straight from your neck to your arms, then bind off straight across each piece. If your shoulders are sloped, bind off each piece in steps, working from the armhole side edge in toward the neckline. We suggest that you bind off incrementally over 1" to 2" of rows. Keep in mind that you may need to start your neckline proportionately higher.

✦ *What type of finishing am I comfortable with?* This is a truly important question. The more complicated you make your knitting, the more complicated the finishing may become. Many of us turn our finished pieces over to a professional finisher. Laura insists on doing all of her own finishing, since she has ultimate control over the final product. If you are comfortable with your own skills, jump in and get started.

We hope that our examples enhance your awareness of the freedom that you have. Your body is not a standard. Designers use a set of standard sizes and very few people fit every one of the criteria that we use for calculating patterns. Always check a pattern before starting to be sure that all of the individual piece sizes will work for you. Feel free to change things. Watch how making a change will affect the other pieces that have to match in finishing. Be responsible for your knitting and be in control of making things fit. We all want to make the size that we feel we "normally" would buy. Each magazine and designer uses a different set of sizes and numbers and each adds a different amount of ease to patterns. It is more important to know your body and how much ease you like for the style you are going to make and then adjust the instructions to best fit your needs. Forget the size label—we don't wear tags on the outside of our sweaters. Make it fit and enjoy the compliments!

FEELINGS
GAUGE AND HAND

Selecting a yarn for a pattern is almost as difficult as deciding which candy to buy from a sweets counter. So many yarns and colors, and you must narrow the selection to one, all the while hoping you have made the right choice.

The first step is to create a swatch. The label on the yarn or the pattern you are following will give you a suggested needle size and recommended gauge. With the suggested needle, cast on at least 4" worth of stitches, and keep in mind that you may be working in a stitch with a pattern multiple.

For example, if the suggested gauge is 4.5 sts = 1" on size 8 needles, cast on at least 18 sts (4.5 x 4"), casting on more, if needed, to get to the right multiple plus edge stitches. Work in the pattern stitch for at least 2". Stop to feel the swatch and look at the stitches. Ask yourself: Are they too loose or too tight? Are they even? Are they too soft or too stiff, too limp or too thick? Make the necessary needle adjustments, up or down, to correct what you don't like; if the fabric is too loose, go down several needle sizes; if too tight, go up. If you are fine-tuning, change one needle size and continue until you have at least 3" of knitting that works. Bind off your swatch.

Swatches from top to bottom:
too tight, just right, too loose

Determine the gauge by laying a tape measure or ruler on the swatch, count across the entire swatch, and divide the number of stitches and rows by the inch measurement for each. If there is a fraction involved, round up to the nearest half stitch or row per inch.

Measuring gauge swatch

Right or wrong, always keep your swatches and attach a note card to them with the following information:

+ Yarn name/manufacturing company: Dune by Trendsetter Yarns
+ Grams/yards per ball: 50g/90yds
+ Needle size: 9
+ Stitch used: Ridge st, corrugated rib, stock st
+ Gauge: stitches x rows/inch (3.5 stitches x 6 rows = 1" in pattern measured over a 4" square)

By attaching this card to each of your swatches, you can go back and use them again. We have used ten-year-old swatches to create some of our new sweaters—you just never know.

Swatch notecard

As important as gauge is, the feel or "hand" of a yarn can make a difference in the success of your knitting. One of Laura's favorite stories about her early knitting career was when as a teen, she purchased a spongy, plied bouclé from a weaving store. There was no label, so knowing that gauge was important, she kept making swatches until the gauge matched the pattern she wanted. The gauge matched all right, but the finished vest was so stiff and thick it stood up on its own! Our goal, as always, is not just to have pieces of a sweater that feel good, but also to have a finished sweater that we love to wear.

Consider the following when selecting and combining different yarns to enhance good qualities and mask undesirable ones:

✦ Traditional plied knitting wools are predictable in their behavior because of the way they are twisted, with individual plies twisted in the opposite direction of the finished twist. This cancels any pent-up energy that can lead to biasing and provides a nice elasticity that is pleasant to work on.

✦ Many current novelty yarns have an exciting look, but they can have drawbacks when knit into a fabric. Bouclés can be limp. Rayon and silk stretch over time, and your stitches may appear too loose and uneven. Many novelty yarns have no elasticity—and thus no give on the needle—and tight knitters can find them difficult.

Novelty yarns

✦ If you have yarns with varied gauges and are working a slip-stitch pattern with two-row intervals, gauge differences of up to a half stitch per inch won't matter because one texture is laid over the other. The overall quality of the fabric evens out and compensates for individual gauge differences.

Plied yarns

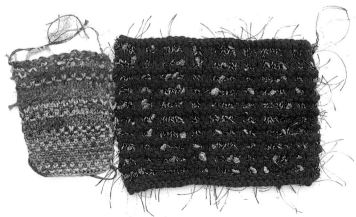

Slip-stitch pattern

Combining a difficult yarn with a well-behaved yarn can improve your knitting and make the experience better. Holding yarns together produces a thicker, overall patterned fabric, such as in "Razzle-Dazzle" (page 128).

Sparkly nylon, thin rayon component with squares of color, and thick spongy nylon yarns held together while knitting

Striping with different yarns or using different types of yarns for A and B in a pattern stitch (page 36) is another way to combine yarns and enhance good qualities while masking undesirable ones. A thinner knit fabric is created and the subtle stripes become a part of the design.

Same yarns as at left, worked in a stripe pattern

You have lots to think about and the knitting world is your oyster. With the knowledge you have at your hands, pick up some needles and create beauty.

CHANGING THE TONE

TEN TRICKS
FOR CUSTOM KNITS

Now that we have the basics down, let's play with ways to enhance that blank canvas that is our sweater. From simple tricks, such as stripes, to fancy cables and pattern work, these are the things we love about knitting—the endless possibilities that arise from two simple needles and a length of yarn.

Stripes

THREE-COLOR stripes are easy and fun to do. Cast on with A, then drop A and attach B. Work across with B, then drop B and attach C. Work across with C, and when you get to the end of the row— A is waiting for you! This is great for combining three yarns whose gauges may be different. Pick the needle that suits the middle-range yarn, and the others will compensate. Try this with solids, with hand-dyed and multicolors, and with contrasting textures. It's also a great way to showcase a special

yarn—just combine it with more subdued yarns. The pattern can be simple stockinette or a more complicated textural stitch.

Ridge Stitch: *Multiple of 10*
    Row 1 (WS): *K5, P5; rep from *.
    Row 2: Knit.
    Row 3: *P5, K5; rep from *.
    Row 4: Knit.
    Rep rows 1–4.

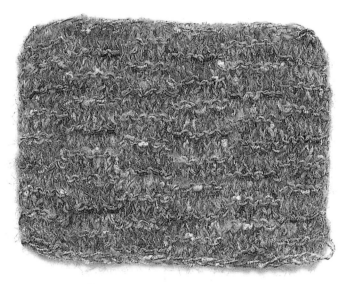

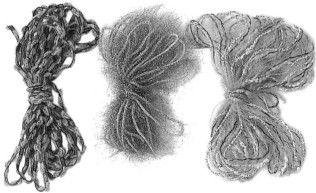

Three different subtle textures in similar colors worked in Ridge stitch.

One-row stripes in stockinette stitch: one solid, two multitextured. Gold is switched for wine halfway through swatch.

Half Linen Stitch

THIS STITCH remains a favorite with us. Relatively simple to knit, it has the virtue of making the fabric a bit denser, which helps to tame many novelty yarns. If a yarn is too limp when knit in stockinette stitch, try the half linen stitch. Worked with multiple colors, either in two-row stripes or in one-row stripes using three colors (see page 36), it serves to blend and mix the colors in an extremely pleasing way.

Half Linen Stitch: *Odd number of stitches*
    Row 1: *K1, sl 1 wyif; rep from *, end K1.
    Row 2: Purl.
    Row 3: K2, *sl 1 wyif, K1; rep from *, end K1.
    Row 4: Purl.
    Rep rows 1–4.

Two rows each of solid and multicolor; top half has the addition of a third yarn for one-row stripes.

Two rows each of two similar multicolors with different textures mix into an allover pattern.

Ribbing

RIB STITCHES add elasticity and produce form-fitting garments. Several variations that include working some rows in garter stitch give the look of rib without being clingy. Wide ribs can add quite a bit of texture and are easy to work, and using uneven numbers of knits and purls is a nice variation. Making ribbed garments in a much larger size will allow the rib to drape and flow.

K3, P3 Rib: *Multiple of 6 plus 3*
>   **Row 1:** *K3, P3; rep from *, end K3.
>   **Row 2:** P3, *K3, P3; rep from *.
>   **Rep rows 1 and 2.**

Mistake Rib: *Odd number of stitches (a wide rib that creates a waffle effect)*
>   **Row 1:** *K2, P2; rep from *.
>   **Row 2:** *K2, P2, rep from *.
>   **Rep rows 1 and 2.**

A mistake rib is a narrow rib that is part seed stitch and thus might not be as elastic.

A wide rib mixes up the colors on one-row stripes of different colors and textures.

Lace Stitches

STITCHES WITH yarnovers add a great deal of interest and are particularly suited to feminine, dressy garments. The openwork can soften a yarn, but really stiff yarns are better worked in another stitch. Lace stitches are particularly nice for mohair and other brushed yarns, where the core shows the stitches but the hair fills in some of the space.

Rickrack Faggoting Stitch: *Multiple of 3 plus 1*
    Row 1 (RS): K1, *YO, SSK, K1; rep from *.
    Row 2: K1, *YO, P2tog, K1; rep from *.
    Rep rows 1 and 2.

Ridged Ribbon Eyelet: *Odd number of stitches*
    Row 1 (RS): Knit.
    Row 2: Purl.
    Rows 3 and 4: Knit.
    Row 5: *K2tog, YO; rep from *, end K1.
    Row 6: Knit.
    Pattern changes to allover lace:
    Row 1 (RS): K1, *YO, K2tog; rep from *.
    Row 2: Purl.
    Row 3: K2, *YO, K2tog; rep from *, end K1.
    Row 4: Purl.
    Rep last 4 rows.

Kid Mohair blended with a bumpy rayon
is worked in an allover lace pattern.

Horizontal ridges and eyelets transform into allover lace.

Simple Slip Stitches

SLIPPING STITCHES is a great way to manipulate color, because the colors both break up and mix together, making this a good choice for multicolored yarn. Because of the slipping, the fabric tends to grow firmer, which can help with limp yarns.

Little Tent Stitch: *Multiple of 8 plus 1*

> **Rows 1 and 3 (WS):** K2, *P5, K3; rep from *, end P5, K2.
>
> **Row 2:** K2, *sl 5 wyif, K3; rep from *, end sl 5 wyif, K2.
>
> **Row 4:** K4, *insert needle under loose strand and knit next st, bringing st out under strand, K7; rep from *, end last rep with K4.
>
> **Rep rows 1–4.**

Garter Ridge Slip Stitch: *Multiple of 5 plus 4*

> **Row 1 (RS):** *K4, sl 1 wyib; rep from *, end K4.
>
> **Row 2:** *K4, P1; rep from *, end K4.
>
> **Rep rows 1 and 2.**

Strong rows of slipped stitches give vertical emphasis to garter stitch.

Yarn carried across the front is picked up and knit in later for rows of diagonal lines.

Knit and Purl Stitches

TEXTURAL COMBINATIONS provide a great deal of interest and are easy to work. Unlike rib stitches, which are knits and purls stacked up on one another, these patterns basically use purl stitches on a ground of knit stitches (or vice versa) to create texture.

Boxed Seed Stitch: *Multiple of 10*

Rows 1, 3, and 5: *P1, K1, P1, K1, P1, K5; rep from *.

Rows 2, 4, and 6: *P5, P1, K1, P1, K1, P1; rep from *.

Rows 7, 9, and 11: *K5, P1, K1, P1, K1, P1; rep from *.

Rows 8, 10, and 12: *P1, K1, P1, K1, P1, K5; rep from *.

Rep rows 1–12.

Seed stitch provides a checkerboard pattern.

Textured Checks: *Multiple of 4 plus 2*

Rows 1: Purl.

Rows 2: Knit.

Rows 3: *K2, P2; rep from *, end K2.

Rows 4: P2, *K2, P2; rep from *.

Rep rows 1–4.

Textured checks look good on either side (swatch changes halfway through).

41

Cables

SIMPLE OR complex, cables can add just the right dash to your knitting recipe. Whether as an allover pattern or a big accent running up a front or sleeves, cables provide deep textural interest. From something as simple as mock cables to elaborate braided strands, think cables!

Eyelet Cable: *Multiple of 5 plus 2*

> **Row 1 (RS):** *P2, K3; rep from *, end P2.
> **Row 2:** *K2, P3; rep from *, end K2.
> **Row 3:** *P2, sl 1 wyib, K2, pass sl st over K2 sts; rep from *, end P2.
> **Row 4:** *K2, P1, YO, P1; rep from *, end K2.
> **Rep rows 1–4.**

Allover Cables: *Multiple of 6 plus 2*

> **Rows 1, 3, and 7:** *P2, K4; rep from *, end P2.
> **Rows 2, 4, and 6:** *K2, P4; rep from *, end K2.
> **Row 5:** *P2, sl 2 sts to cn and hold in front, K2, K2 from cn; rep from *, end P2.
> **Row 8:** *K2, P4; rep from *, end K2.
> **Rep rows 1–8.**

A cable variation that incorporates eyelets and doesn't use a cable needle.

Cables worked in an allover pattern.

Chevron Stitches

LOTS OF energy grows from chevron stitches with their playful zigzags. Great for multicolored yarns, they show stripes in a new way. Whether you or the yarns add extra color, worked in either garter or stockinette stitch, chevrons give you good options for interest.

Large Gauge Chevron Stitch: *Multiple of 10 plus 3*
    Row 1: K1, SSK, *K3, YO, K1, YO, K3, sl 2
        tog as if to knit, K1, p2sso; rep from *,
        end K3, YO, K1, YO, K3, K2tog, K1.
    Row 2: Purl (for stockinette fabric) *or* knit
        (for garter fabric).
    Rep rows 1 and 2.

Garter Chevron: *Multiple of 16 plus 3*
    Row 1: K1, *K1, YO, K6, sl 1 wyib, K2tog,
        psso, K6, YO; rep from *, end K2.
    Row 2: K2, *P1, K13, P2; rep from *,
        end K1.
    Rep rows 1 and 2.

Solid stripes banded with a multicolored texture
add interest to this large garter chevron.

You can change the look of a single multicolored
yarn in garter stitch (bottom) by switching to
stockinette stitch and alternating every two rows
with another yarn (top).

Color Work

THE PROVINCE of knitters and artists alike—using more than one color—provides the perfect enhancement to our blank canvas. Modern computer programs for charts allow your color work to get as elaborate as you wish, but here we show you several simple ways of working with color.

Fair Isle Stitch: *Multiple of 6 plus 2 with yarns A and B*

> **Rows 1 and 3:** K1 with B, *K3 with A, K3 with B; rep from *, end K1 with A.
>
> **Rows 2 and 4:** P1 with A, *P3 with B, P3 with A; rep from *, end P1 with B.
>
> **Rows 5 and 7:** K1 with A, *K3 with B, K3 with A; rep from *, end K1 with B.
>
> **Rows 6 and 8:** P1 with B, *P3 with A, P3 with B; rep from*, end P1 with A.
>
> **Rep rows 1–8.**

Solid and multicolored yarns make the checkerboard appear and disappear.

Yarn Creation

BECOME YOUR own yarn designer! Knitting with more than one yarn held together throughout the garment lets you use even the thinnest yarns. Think thick and chunky; generally, the gauge is going to get larger and so will the needle. If you have a problem yarn, think about combining it with something else.

Worked in stockinette stitch, a soft furry nylon paired with a sparkly nylon improves both (bottom). The fur softens both the look and hand of the sparkle, and together they are firmer than each is separately. The top half shows the switch to a nubby rayon instead of the sparkle.

THE TEMPLATES
YOUR GUIDES TO GREAT KNITS

You've taken measurements and determined a size. You've also made a swatch with your selected yarn and know the appropriate gauge. Now, look through the following pages for your gauge, and find the column with your size. Following the column down, enter the numbers for your size onto the Blank Pattern Worksheet (pages 19–20) at the corresponding letters. Make any allowances for borders, pattern-stitch multiples, and adjustments for a custom fit. The swatch at the right side of each gauge chart is a full-size representation of the stitches per inch for that gauge.

Gauge (2 sts x 3 rows = 1")

Finished Bust/Chest	30	32	34	36	38	40	42
½ BODY (Back)							
A) CO Straight Body	30	32	34	36	38	40	42
A) CO Cropped Shape Taper	26	28	30	32	34	36	38
B) Inc 1 ea end every ___ rows ___ times	14/2	14/2	14/2	14/2	14/2	14/2	14/2
A) CO Fingertip Taper	34	36	38	40	42	44	46
C) Dec 1 ea end every ___" ___ times	8/2	8/2	8/2	8/2	8/2	9/2	9/2
A) CO Long Taper	38	40	44	46	48	50	52
C) Dec 1 ea end every ___" ___ times	6/4	6/4	6/5	6/5	6/5	6/5	6/5
SHAPE ARMHOLE							
Cut In (sleeveless)							
E) BO ___ sts beg next ___ rows	2/2	2/2	2/2	2/2	2/2	3/2	3/2
F) Dec 1 ea end EOR ___ times	1	1	2	2	3	3	4
G) Dec 1 ea end every 4th row ___ times	1	1	1	2	2	2	2
Set In							
E) BO ___ sts beg next ___ rows	2/2	2/2	2/2	2/2	2/2	2/2	2/2
F) Dec 1 ea end EOR ___ times	1	1	2	2	3	4	5
Modified Drop							
H) BO ___ sts beg next 2 rows	2	2	2	3	3	4	4
½ BODY (Pullover Front)							
Boat Neck: (J) BO ctr ___ sts	16	16	16	16	18	18	18
Round Neck Shaping							
K) BO ctr ___ sts	4	4	4	4	4	4	4
L) BO ___ sts ea neck edge 1 time	2	2	2	2	2	2	2
M) BO ___ sts ea neck edge 1 time	0	0	0	0	0	0	0
N) Dec 1 ea neck edge EOR ___ times	1	1	1	1	2	2	2
Deep V: Dec ea neck edge							
O) every ___ rows ___ times	4/5	4/5	4/5	4/5	4/6	4/6	4/6
Shallow V: Dec ea neck edge							
O) every ___ rows ___ times	2/5	2/5	2/5	2/5	2/6	2/6	2/6
½ FRONT (Cardigan/Jkt)							
P) CO Straight Shape	15	16	17	18	19	20	21
P) CO Fingertip Taper	17	18	19	20	21	22	23
Q) Dec 1 at side edge every ___" ___ times	8/2	8/2	8/2	8/2	8/2	9/2	9/2
P) CO Long Taper	19	20	22	23	24	25	26
Q) Dec 1 at side edge every ___" ___ times	6/4	6/4	6/5	6/5	6/5	6/5	6/5
Round Neck Shaping							
R) BO ___ sts beg next 2 rows.	2	2	2	2	2	2	2
Follow shaping (L,M,N) from above							
SLEEVES							
S) CO Long Sleeve	12	12	12	14	14	14	14
T) Inc 1 ea end every ___ rows ___ times	6/7	6/7	6/8	7/6	8/6	6/8	6/8
S) CO Short Sleeve	20	20	22	22	22	24	24
T) Inc 1 ea end every ___ rows ___ times	3/3	3/3	3/3	3/3	4/3	4/3	4/3
S) CO Cap Sleeve	24	24	26	26	26	28	28
T) Inc 1 ea end every ___ rows ___ times	3/1	3/1	3/1	3/1	4/1	4/1	4/1
CAP SHAPING							
Set In							
U) BO ___ sts beg next 2 rows	2	2	2	2	2	2	2
V) Dec 1 ea end EOR for ___"	4	4	4	4.5	4.5	4.5	5
Modified Drop							
W) BO ___ sts beg every row ___ times	2/10	2/10	2/10	2/10	2/10	2/10	2/10

44	46	48	50	52	54	56	58	60
44	46	48	50	52	54	56	58	60
40	40	43	44	46	48	50	52	54
14/2	10/3	10/3	10/3	10/3	10/3	10/3	10/3	10/3
48	52	54	56	58	60	62	64	66
9/2	6/3	6/3	6/3	6/3	7/3	7/3	7/3	7/3
54	56	58	60	64	66	68	70	72
6/5	6/5	6/5	6/5	5/6	5/6	5/6	5/6	5/6
3/2	2/4	3/4	3/4	3/4	3/4	3/4	3/4	3/4
5	5	4	4	6	7	9	9	10
2	2	2	2	1	1	0	0	0
2/2	3/2	3/2	3/2	3/2	3/2	3/2	3/2	3/2
5	5	5	5	6	7	8	8	9
5	5	5	5	6	6	7	7	8
18	18	18	20	20	20	20	20	20
4	4	4	4	4	4	4	4	4
2	2	2	2	2	2	2	2	2
0	0	2	2	2	2	2	2	2
2	2	1	1	1	1	1	1	1
4/6	4/6	3/7	3/7	3/7	3/7	4/7	4/7	4/7
2/6	2/6	2/6	2/7	2/7	2/7	2/7	2/7	2/7
22	23	24	25	26	27	28	29	30
24	26	27	28	29	30	31	32	33
9/2	6/3	6/3	6/3	6/3	7/3	7/3	7/3	7/3
27	28	29	30	32	33	34	35	36
6/5	6/5	6/5	6/5	5/6	5/6	5/6	5/6	5/6
2	2	2	2	2	2	2	2	2
15	16	16	17	18	18	18	18	18
6/8	6/8	6/8	6/8	6/8	6/8	6/9	6/9	6/9
25	26	26	27	28	28	30	30	30
4/3	4/3	4/3	4/3	4/3	4/3	4/3	4/3	4/3
29	30	30	31	32	32	32	32	32
4/1	4/1	4/1	4/1	4/1	4/1	3/2	3/2	3/2
2	3	3	3	3	3	3	3	3
5	5	5.5	5.5	5.5	6	6	6.5	6.5
2 /10	3/10	3/10	3/10	3/10	3/10	3/10	3/10	3/10

47

Gauge (2.5 sts x 3 rows = 1")

Finished Bust/Chest	30	32	34	36	38	40	42
½ BODY (Back)							
A) CO Straight Body	38	40	42	46	48	50	54
A) CO Cropped Shape Taper	34	36	38	42	44	46	48
B) Inc 1 ea end every ___ rows ___ times	16/2	16/2	16/2	16/2	16/2	16/2	12/3
A) CO Fingertip Taper	42	44	46	50	52	54	60
C) Dec 1 ea end every ___" ___ times	8/2	8/2	8/2	8/2	8/2	8/2	6/3
A) CO Long Taper	48	50	54	58	60	62	66
C) Dec 1 ea end every ___" ___ times	6/5	6/5	5/6	5/6	5/6	5/6	5/6
SHAPE ARMHOLE							
Cut In (sleeveless)							
E) BO ___sts beg next ___ rows	2/2	2/2	3/2	3/2	3/2	3/2	4/2
F) Dec 1 ea end EOR ___ times	2	3	3	3	4	4	4
G) Dec 1 ea end every 4th row ___ times	2	2	2	3	3	3	4
Set In							
E) BO ___sts beg next ___ rows	2/2	2/2	2/2	2/2	2/2	3/2	3/2
F) Dec 1 ea end EOR ___ times	1	2	2	4	4	4	6
Modified Drop							
H) BO ___sts beg next 2 rows	2	2	2	4	4	5	6
½ BODY (Pullover Front)							
Boat Neck: (J) BO ctr ___sts	20	20	20	20	22	22	22
Round Neck Shaping							
K) BO ctr ___sts	6	6	6	6	6	6	6
L) BO ___sts ea neck edge 1 time	2	2	2	2	2	2	2
M) BO ___sts ea neck edge 1 time	0	0	0	0	0	0	2
N) Dec 1 ea neck edge EOR ___ times	1	1	2	2	2	2	1
Deep V: Dec ea neck edge							
O) every ___ rows ___ times	4/6	4/6	3/7	3/7	3/7	3/7	3/8
Shallow V: Dec ea neck edge							
O) every ___ rows ___ times	2/6	2/6	2/7	2/7	2/7	2/7	2/8
½ FRONT (Cardigan/Jkt)							
P) CO Straight Shape	19	20	21	23	24	25	27
P) CO Fingertip Taper	21	22	23	25	26	27	30
Q) Dec 1 at side edge every ___" ___ times	8/2	8/2	8/2	8/2	8/2	8/2	6/3
P) CO Long Taper	24	25	27	29	30	31	33
Q) Dec 1 at side edge every ___" ___ times	6/5	6/5	5/6	5/6	5/6	5/6	5/6
Round Neck Shaping							
R) BO ___sts beg next 2 rows.	3	3	3	3	3	3	3
Follow shaping (L,M,N) from above							
SLEEVES							
S) CO Long Sleeve	15	15	16	16	17	18	18
T) Inc 1 ea end every ___ rows ___ times	5/9	5/10	5/10	5/10	5/10	5/10	5/10
S) CO Short Sleeve	25	25	26	26	27	28	30
T) Inc 1 ea end every ___ rows ___ times	3/4	2/5	2/5	2/5	2/5	2/5	3/4
S) CO Cap Sleeve	29	31	32	32	33	34	36
T) Inc 1 ea end every ___ rows ___ times	2/2	2/2	2/2	2/2	2/2	2/2	4/1
CAP SHAPING							
Set In							
U) BO ___sts beg next 2 rows	2	2	2	2	2	3	3
V) Dec 1 ea end EOR for ___"	4	4	4	4.5	4.5	4.5	5
Modified Drop							
W) BO ___sts beg every row ___ times	2/10	2/10	2/10	2/10	2/10	2/10	3/10

44	46	48	50	52	54	56	58	60
56	58	60	62	66	68	70	72	76
50	52	54	56	58	60	62	64	68
12/3	12/3	12/3	12/3	10/4	10/4	10/4	10/4	10/4
62	64	66	68	74	76	78	80	84
6/3	6/3	6/3	6/3	5/4	5/4	5/4	5/4	5/4
68	72	74	76	80	82	86	88	92
5/6	4/7	4/7	4/7	4/7	4/7	4/8	4/8	4/8
5/2	5/2	4/4	4/4	4/4	5/4	5/4	4/4	4/4
4	4	3	4	4	4	4	3	4
4	4	3	3	4	3	3	3	3
3/2	3/2	3/2	3/2	2/4	2/4	3/4	3/4	3/4
6	7	7	7	8	8	7	7	8
7	6	6	6	8	8	9	9	10
22	22	22	24	24	24	24	26	26
6	6	6	6	6	6	6	6	6
2	2	2	2	3	3	3	3	3
2	2	2	2	2	2	2	2	2
1	1	1	1	1	1	1	1	1
3/8	3/8	3/8	3/8	3/9	3/9	3/9	3/9	3/9
2/8	2/8	2/8	2/8	2/9	2/9	2/9	2/9	2/9
28	29	30	31	33	34	35	36	38
31	32	33	34	37	38	39	40	42
6/3	6/3	6/3	6/3	5/4	5/4	5/4	5/4	5/4
34	36	37	38	40	41	43	44	46
5/6	4/7	4/7	4/7	4/7	4/7	4/8	4/8	4/8
3	3	3	3	3	3	3	3	3
20	20	20	20	22	22	22	24	24
5/10	5/10	5/10	5/10	5/10	5/10	5/11	5/11	5/11
32	32	32	34	34	36	36	38	38
3/4	3/4	4/4	4/4	4/4	4/4	4/4	4/4	4/4
38	38	38	40	40	40	40	40	40
4/1	4/1	4/1	6/1	6/1	6/1	4/2	3/3	3/3
3	3	3	3	3	3	3	3	3
5	5	5.5	5.5	5.5	6	6	6.5	6.5
3/10	3/10	3/10	3/10	3/10	3/10	3/12	3/12	3/12

Gauge (3 sts x 5 rows = 1")

Finished Bust/Chest	30	32	34	36	38	40	42
½ BODY (Back)							
A) CO Straight Body	46	48	52	54	58	60	64
A) CO Cropped Shape Taper	40	44	46	48	52	54	58
B) Inc 1 ea end every ___ rows ___ times	17/3	22/2	16/3	16/3	16/3	16/3	16/3
A) CO Fingertip Taper	50	52	56	60	64	66	70
C) Dec 1 ea end every ___" ___ times	8.5/2	8.5/2	9/2	6/3	6.5/3	6/3	6/3
A) CO Long Taper	58	62	64	68	72	76	78
C) Dec 1 ea end every ___" ___ times	4.5/6	4/7	5/6	4/7	4/7	3.5/8	4/7
SHAPE ARMHOLE							
Cut In (sleeveless)							
E) BO ___sts beg next ___ rows	2/2	3/2	3/2	3/2	4/2	4/2	4/2
F) Dec 1 ea end EOR ___ times	2	2	3	4	4	4	5
G) Dec 1 ea end every 4th row ___ times	2	2	3	3	4	4	5
Set In							
E) BO ___sts beg next ___ rows	2/2	2/2	2/2	3/2	3/2	3/2	4/2
F) Dec 1 ea end EOR ___ times	2	2	4	4	5	6	6
Modified Drop							
H) BO ___sts beg next 2 rows	2	3	3	4	5	6	6
½ BODY (Pullover Front)							
Boat Neck: (J) BO ctr ___sts	24	24	24	24	26	26	26
Round Neck Shaping							
K) BO ctr ___sts	6	6	6	6	8	8	8
L) BO ___sts ea neck edge 1 time	2	2	2	2	2	2	2
M) BO ___sts ea neck edge 1 time	2	2	2	2	2	2	2
N) Dec 1 ea neck edge EOR ___ times	1	1	1	1	1	1	1
Deep V: Dec ea neck edge							
O) every ___ rows ___ times	4/8	4/8	4/8	4/8	4/9	4/9	4/9
Shallow V: Dec ea neck edge							
O) every ___ rows ___ times	2/8	2/8	2/8	3/8	2/9	2/9	2/9
½ FRONT (Cardigan/Jkt)							
P) CO Straight Shape	23	24	26	27	29	30	32
P) CO Fingertip Taper	25	26	28	30	32	33	35
Q) Dec 1 at side edge every ___" ___ times	8.5/2	8.5/2	9/2	6/3	6.5/3	6/3	6/3
P) CO Long Taper	29	31	32	34	36	38	39
Q) Dec 1 at side edge every ___" ___ times	4.5/6	4/7	5/6	4/17	4/7	3.5/8	4/7
Round Neck Shaping							
R) BO ___sts beg next 2 rows.	3	3	3	3	4	4	4
Follow shaping (L,M,N) from above							
SLEEVES							
S) CO Long Sleeve	18	18	18	20	22	22	22
T) Inc 1 ea end every ___ rows ___ times	6/11	6/11	6/12	6/11	6/11	6/12	6/12
S) CO Short Sleeve	30	30	32	34	34	36	36
T) Inc 1 ea end every ___ rows ___ times	3/5	3/5	3/5	4/4	3/5	3/5	3/5
S) CO Cap Sleeve	36	36	38	38	40	42	42
T) Inc 1 ea end every ___ rows ___ times	3/2	3/2	3/2	3/2	3/2	3/2	3/2
CAP SHAPING							
Set In							
U) BO ___sts beg next 2 rows	2	2	2	3	3	3	4
V) Dec 1 ea end EOR for ___"	4	4	4	4.5	4.5	4.5	5
Modified Drop							
W) BO ___sts beg every row ___ times	2/14	2/14	2/14	2/14	2/14	2/16	2/16

44	46	48	50	52	54	56	58	60
66	70	72	76	78	82	84	88	90
60	62	66	68	70	74	76	80	82
16/3	13/4	15/3	13/4	13/4	13/4	13/4	13/4	13/4
72	76	80	82	86	88	92	94	98
6/3	6/3	5/4	6.5/3	5/4	6.5/3	5/4	6.5/3	5/4
82	86	88	92	94	98	102	106	108
3.5/8	3.5/8	3.5/8	3.5/8	3.5/8	4/8	3.5/9	3.5/9	3.5/9
5/2	5/2	6/2	6/2	4/4	5/4	5/4	6/6	6/6
5	6	6	6	6	6	6	6	6
5	5	5	6	5	5	6	5	6
4/2	5/2	5/2	6/2	6/2	4/4	4/4	5/4	5/4
6	7	7	7	7	7	7	7	8
7	8	7	8	9	9	10	11	12
26	26	28	28	28	30	30	30	30
10	10	10	10	10	10	10	12	12
2	2	2	2	2	2	2	2	2
2	2	2	2	2	2	2	2	2
1	1	1	2	2	2	2	2	2
4/10	4/10	4/10	4/11	4/11	4/11	4/11	4/12	4/12
2/10	2/10	2/10	2/11	2/11	2/11	2/11	2/12	2/12
33	35	36	38	39	41	42	44	45
36	38	40	41	43	44	46	47	49
6/3	6/3	5/4	6.5/3	5/4	6.5/3	5/4	6.5/3	5/4
41	43	44	46	47	49	51	53	54
3.5/8	3.5/8	3.5/8	3.5/8	3.5/8	4/8	3.5/9	3.5/9	3.5/9
5	5	5	5	5	5	5	6	6
24	24	24	26	26	28	28	28	30
6/12	6/12	6/12	6/12	6/13	6/12	6/13	6/13	7/12
38	40	40	42	42	42	44	46	46
3/5	4/4	5/4	5/4	4/5	4/5	4/5	5/4	5/4
44	46	46	48	48	48	48	50	50
3/2	4/1	6/1	6/1	4/2	4/2	4/3	5/2	5/2
4	5	5	6	6	4	4	5	5
5	5	5.5	5.5	5.5	6	6	6.5	6.5
2/16	2/16	2/16	2/16	2/16	2/16	3/14	3/14	3/14

Gauge (3.5 sts x 5 rows = 1")

Finished Bust/Chest	30	32	34	36	38	40	42
½ BODY (Back)							
A) CO Straight Body	52	56	60	64	66	70	74
A) CO Cropped Shape Taper	48	50	54	56	60	64	66
B) Inc 1 ea end every ___ rows ___ times	24/2	18/3	20/3	14/4	20/3	20/3	14/4
A) CO Fingertip Taper	58	62	66	70	74	78	80
C) Dec 1 ea end every ___" ___ times	6/3	6/3	6/3	6/3	5/4	5/4	6/3
A) CO Long Taper	68	72	76	80	84	88	92
C) Dec 1 ea end every ___" ___ times	3/8	3/8	3/8	3/8	3/9	3/9	3/9
SHAPE ARMHOLE							
Cut In (sleeveless)							
E) BO ___ sts beg next ___ rows.	3/2	3/2	4/2	4/2	5/2	5/2	3/4
F) Dec 1 ea end EOR ___ times	2	3	3	4	4	5	5
G) Dec 1 ea end every 4th row ___ times	2	3	3	4	4	4	5
Set In							
E) BO ___ sts beg next ___ rows	2/2	2/2	3/2	4/2	4/2	5/2	5/2
F) Dec 1 ea end EOR ___ times	2	3	3	4	4	5	7
Modified Drop							
H) BO ___ sts beg next 2 rows	2	3	4	6	5	7	7
½ BODY (Pullover Front)							
Boat Neck: (J) BO ctr ___ sts	28	28	28	28	30	30	32
Round Neck Shaping							
K) BO ctr ___ sts	8	8	10	10	10	10	10
L) BO ___ sts ea neck edge 1 time	2	2	2	2	3	3	3
M) BO ___ sts ea neck edge 1 time	2	2	2	2	2	2	2
N) Dec 1 ea neck edge EOR ___ times	1	1	1	1	1	1	1
Deep V: Dec ea neck edge							
O) every ___ rows ___ times	4/9	4/9	4/10	4/10	4/11	4/11	4/11
Shallow V: Dec ea neck edge							
O) every ___ rows ___ times	2/9	2/9	2/10	2/10	2/11	2/11	2/11
½ FRONT (Cardigan/Jkt)							
P) CO Straight Shape	26	28	30	32	33	35	37
P) CO Fingertip Taper	29	31	33	35	37	39	40
Q) Dec 1 at side edge every ___" ___ times	6/3	6/3	6/3	6/3	5/4	5/4	6/3
P) CO Long Taper	34	36	38	40	42	44	46
Q) Dec 1 at side edge every ___" ___ times	3/8	3/8	3/8	3/8	3/9	3/9	3/9
Round Neck Shaping							
R) BO ___ sts beg next 2 rows.	4	4	5	5	5	5	6
Follow shaping (L,M,N) from above							
SLEEVES							
S) CO Long Sleeve	22	22	22	24	24	24	24
T) Inc 1 ea end every ___ rows ___ times	6/12	6/12	6/13	6/13	6/13	6/14	6/14
S) CO Short Sleeve	36	36	38	38	38	40	42
T) Inc 1 ea end every ___ rows ___ times	4/5	4/5	4/5	3/6	3/6	3/6	4/5
S) CO Cap Sleeve	42	42	44	46	46	48	48
T) Inc 1 ea end every ___ rows ___ times	3/2	3/2	3/2	3/2	4/2	4/2	4/2
CAP SHAPING							
Set In							
U) BO ___ sts beg next 2 rows	2	2	3	4	4	5	5
V) Dec 1 ea end EOR for ___"	4	4	4	4.5	4.5	4.5	5
Modified Drop							
W) BO ___ sts beg every row ___ times	2/16	2/16	2/16	2/16	2/16	2/16	2/16

44	46	48	50	52	54	56	58	60
78	80	84	88	92	94	98	102	106
70	72	76	78	82	86	90	94	96
14/4	14/4	14/4	14/5	14/5	14/4	14/4	14/4	12/5
84	88	92	96	100	104	106	110	114
6/3	5/4	5/4	5/4	5/4	4/5	5/4	5/4	5/4
94	100	104	106	110	114	118	122	126
3.5/8	3/10	3/10	3/9	3.5/9	3/10	3.5/10	3/10	3.5/10
4/4	4/4	5/4	5/4	5/4	5/4	6/4	4/6	5/6
5	5	5	6	6	8	8	9	8
5	5	5	5	5	5	5	5	5
5/2	5/2	5/2	5/2	3/4	3/4	4/4	4/4	5/4
8	8	9	10	10	10	10	11	11
9	8	9	9	11	11	12	12	14
32	32	32	34	34	34	34	36	36
10	10	10	12	12	12	12	12	12
3	3	3	3	3	3	3	3	3
2	2	2	2	2	2	2	2	2
1	1	1	1	1	1	1	1	1
4/11	4/11	4/11	4/12	4/12	4/12	4/12	4/12	4/12
2/11	2/11	2/11	2/12	2/12	2/12	2/12	2/12	2/12
39	40	42	44	46	47	49	51	53
42	44	46	48	50	52	53	55	57
6/3	5/4	5/4	5/4	5/4	4/5	5/4	5/4	5/4
47	50	52	53	55	57	59	61	63
3.5/8	3/10	3/10	3/9	3.5/9	3/10	3.5/10	3/10	3.5/10
6	5	5	6	6	6	6	6	6
26	28	28	30	30	32	32	32	32
6/14	6/14	6/14	6/14	5/15	6/14	6/15	5/16	5/16
44	46	46	48	50	50	52	52	52
4/5	4/5	4/5	4/5	4/5	4/5	5/5	4/6	4/6
50	52	52	54	56	56	56	58	58
4/2	4/2	5/2	5/2	5/2	5/2	4/3	4/3	4/3
5	5	5	5	3	3	4	4	5
5	5	5.5	5.5	5.5	6	6	6.5	6.5
2/16	2/16	2/16	2/16	2/16	2/16	3/16	3/16	3/16

Gauge (4 sts x 6.5 rows = 1")

Finished Bust/Chest	30	32	34	36	38	40	42
½ BODY (Back)							
A) CO Straight Body	60	64	68	72	76	80	84
A) CO Cropped Shape Taper	54	58	62	64	68	72	76
B) Inc 1 ea end every ___ rows ___ times	20/3	20/3	20/3	14/4	14/4	14/4	14/4
A) CO Fingertip Taper	66	70	74	80	84	88	92
C) Dec 1 ea end every ___" ___ times	5.5/3	5.5/8	6/3	4.5/4	4.5/4	4.5/4	4.5/4
A) CO Long Taper	78	82	86	92	96	100	104
C) Dec 1 ea end every ___" ___ times	3/9	3/9	3.5/9	2.5/10	2.5/10	2.5/10	2.5/10
SHAPE ARMHOLE							
Cut In (sleeveless)							
E) BO ___sts beg next ___ rows	3/2	4/2	4/2	5/2	5/2	6/2	6/2
F) Dec 1 ea end EOR ___ times	3	3	4	4	5	5	6
G) Dec 1 ea end every 4th row ___ times	2	3	3	4	5	5	6
Set In							
E) BO ___sts beg next ___ rows	3/2	3/2	3/2	4/2	5/2	5/2	6/2
F) Dec 1 ea end EOR ___ times	2	3	4	5	5	7	7
Modified Drop							
H) BO ___sts beg next 2 rows	2	4	4	6	6	8	8
½ BODY (Pullover Front)							
Boat Neck: (J) BO ctr ___sts	32	32	32	32	34	34	34
Round Neck Shaping							
K) BO ctr ___sts	6	6	8	8	10	10	10
L) BO ___sts ea neck edge 1 time	3	3	3	3	3	3	3
M) BO ___sts ea neck edge 1 time	2	2	2	2	2	2	2
N) Dec 1 ea neck edge EOR ___ times	2	2	2	2	2	2	2
Deep V: Dec ea neck edge							
O) every ___ rows ___ times	4/10	4/10	4/11	4/11	4/12	4/12	4/13
Shallow V: Dec ea neck edge							
O) every ___ rows ___ times	3/10	3/10	3/11	3/11	3/12	3/12	3/12
½ FRONT (Cardigan/Jkt)							
P) CO Straight Shape	30	32	34	36	38	40	42
P) CO Fingertip Taper	33	35	37	40	42	44	46
Q) Dec 1 at side edge every ___" ___ times	5.5/3	5.5/3	6/3	4.5/4	4.5/4	4.5/4	4.5/4
P) CO Long Taper	39	41	43	46	48	50	52
Q) Dec 1 at side edge every ___" ___ times	3/9	3/9	3.5/9	2.5/10	2.5/10	2.5/10	2.5/10
Round Neck Shaping							
R) BO ___sts beg next 2 rows.	3	3	4	4	5	5	5
Follow shaping (L,M,N) from above							
SLEEVES							
S) CO Long Sleeve	24	24	24	28	28	28	28
T) Inc 1 ea end every ___ rows ___ times	6/14	6/14	6/16	6/14	6/14	6/16	6/16
S) CO Short Sleeve	40	40	44	44	44	48	48
T) Inc 1ea end every ___ rows ___ times	4/6	4/6	4/6	4/6	4/6	4/6	4/6
S) CO Cap Sleeve	48	48	52	52	52	56	56
T) Inc 1ea end every ___ rows ___ times	4/2	4/2	4/2	4/2	4/2	4/2	4/2
CAP SHAPING							
Set In							
U) BO ___sts beg next 2 rows	3	3	3	4	5	5	6
V) Dec 1 ea end EOR for ___"	4	4	4	4.5	4.5	4.5	5
Modified Drop							
W) BO ___sts beg every row ___ times	2/20	2/20	2/20	2/20	2/20	2/20	2/20

44	46	48	50	52	54	56	58	60
88	92	96	100	104	108	112	116	120
80	82	86	90	94	98	102	106	110
14/4	12/5	12/5	12/5	12/5	12/5	12/5	12/5	12/5
96	102	106	110	114	118	122	126	130
4.5/4	4/5	4/5	4/5	4/5	4/5	4/5	4.5/5	4.5/5
108	114	118	122	126	130	136	140	144
3/10	2.5/11	2.5/11	3/11	3/11	3/11	2.5/12	3/12	3/12
6/2	7/2	4/4	4/4	4/4	5/4	6/4	6/4	7/4
7	7	8	8	10	9	9	9	10
7	7	7	8	8	8	8	9	9
6/2	6/2	4/4	4/4	5/4	5/4	6/4	6/4	7/4
8	9	8	9	8	9	9	10	10
10	10	10	10	12	12	14	14	16
36	36	36	38	38	38	38	40	40
10	12	12	12	12	12	12	12	12
3	3	3	3	3	3	3	3	3
2	2	2	2	2	2	2	2	2
2	2	2	2	3	3	3	3	3
4/12	4/13	4/13	4/13	4/14	4/14	4/14	4/14	4/14
3/12	2/13	2/13	2/13	2/14	2/14	2/14	2/14	2/14
44	46	48	50	52	54	56	58	60
48	51	53	55	57	59	61	63	65
4.5/4	4/5	4/5	4/5	4/5	4/5	4/5	4.5/5	4.5/5
54	57	59	61	63	65	68	70	72
3/10	2.5/11	2.5/11	3/11	3/11	3/11	2.5/12	3/12	3/12
5	6	6	6	6	6	6	6	6
32	32	32	36	36	36	36	36	36
6/16	6/16	6/16	6/16	6/16	6/16	6/18	6/18	6/18
52	52	52	56	56	56	60	60	60
4/6	4/6	4/6	4/6	4/6	4/6	4/6	4/6	4/6
60	60	60	64	64	64	64	60	64
4/2	4/2	6/2	6/2	6/2	6/2	4/4	4/4	4/4
6	6	4	4	5	5	6	6	7
5	5	5.5	5.5	5.5	6	6	6.5	6.5
3/18	3/18	3/18	3/18	3/18	3/18	3/18	3/18	3/18

Gauge (4.5 sts x 7 rows = 1")

Finished Bust/Chest	30	32	34	36	38	40	42
½ BODY (Back)							
A) CO Straight Body	68	72	76	82	86	90	94
A) CO Cropped Shape Taper	60	64	68	72	76	80	84
B) Inc 1 ea end every ___ rows ___ times	16/4	16/4	16/4	14/5	14/5	14/5	14/5
A) CO Fingertip Taper	74	78	82	90	94	98	102
C) Dec 1 ea end every ___" ___ times	6/3	6/3	6/3	4.5/4	4.5/4	4.5/4	4.5/4
A) CO Long Taper	88	92	96	104	108	112	116
C) Dec 1 ea end every ___" ___ times	2.5/10	2.5/10	2.5/10	2.5/11	2.5/11	2.5/11	2.5/11
SHAPE ARMHOLE							
Cut In (sleeveless)							
E) BO ___sts beg next ___ rows	4/2	5/2	5/2	5/2	5/2	5/2	5/2
F) Dec 1 ea end EOR ___ times	3	3	4	5	6	7	8
G) Dec 1 ea end every 4th row ___ times	2	3	3	5	6	6	7
Set In							
E) BO ___sts beg next ___ rows	3/2	4/2	4/2	5/2	5/2	5/2	5/2
F) Dec 1 ea end EOR ___ times	3	3	4	6	7	9	10
Modified Drop							
H) BO ___sts beg next 2 rows	3	4	4	7	7	9	9
½ BODY (Pullover Front)							
Boat Neck: (J) BO ctr ___sts	36	36	36	36	38	38	40
Round Neck Shaping							
K) BO ctr ___sts	10	10	12	12	12	12	14
L) BO ___sts ea neck edge 1 time	3	3	3	3	3	3	3
M) BO ___sts ea neck edge 1 time	2	2	2	2	3	2	2
N) Dec 1 ea neck edge EOR ___ times	1	1	1	1	2	2	2
Deep V: Dec ea neck edge							
O) every ___ rows ___ times	4/11	4/11	4/12	4/12	4/13	4/13	4/14
Shallow V: Dec ea neck edge							
O) every ___ rows ___ times	2/11	2/11	2/12	3/12	2/13	2/13	2/14
½ FRONT (Cardigan/Jkt)							
P) CO Straight Shape	34	36	38	41	43	45	47
P) CO Fingertip Taper	37	39	41	45	47	49	51
Q) Dec 1 at side edge every ___" ___ times	6/3	6/3	6/3	4.5/4	4.5/4	4.5/4	4.5/4
P) CO Long Taper	44	46	48	52	54	56	58
Q) Dec 1 at side edge every ___" ___ times	2.5/10	2.5/10	2.5/10	2.5/11	2.5/11	2.5/11	2.5/11
Round Neck Shaping							
R) BO ___sts beg next 2 rows.	11	11	12	12	13	13	14
Follow shaping (L,M,N) from above							
SLEEVES							
S) CO Long Sleeve	26	28	28	30	32	32	34
T) Inc 1 ea end every ___ rows ___ times	6/16	6/16	6/17	6/17	6/17	6/18	6/18
S) CO Short Sleeve	44	46	48	50	52	54	56
T) Inc 1ea end every ___ rows ___ times	4/7	4/7	4/7	4/7	4/7	4/7	4/7
S) CO Cap Sleeve	54	56	58	60	62	64	66
T) Inc 1ea end every ___ rows ___ times	4/2	4/2	4/2	4/2	6/2	6/2	6/2
CAP SHAPING							
Set In							
U) BO ___sts beg next 2 rows	3	4	4	5	5	5	5
V) Dec 1 ea end EOR for ___"	4	4	4	4.5	4.5	4.5	5
Modified Drop							
W) BO ___sts beg every row ___ times	2/20	2/20	2/20	2/20	2/20	2/20	2/20

44	46	48	50	52	54	56	58	60
100	104	108	112	118	122	126	130	136
90	94	98	102	108	112	116	120	126
14/5	14/5	14/5	14/5	14/5	14/5	14/5	14/5	14/5
110	114	118	122	128	132	136	140	146
4/5	4/5	4/5	4/5	4/5	4/5	4/5	4/5	4/5
124	128	134	138	144	148	154	158	164
2.5/12	2.5/12	2/13	2/13	2/13	2.5/13	2/14	2/14	2/14
4/4	5/4	5/4	5/4	6/4	6/4	6/6	6/6	6/6
8	7	9	9	11	12	8	8	10
7	7	8	8	7	7	7	8	8
6/2	6/2	5/4	5/4	5/4	6/4	6/4	6/4	6/4
10	11	8	9	10	10	12	13	15
11	12	11	11	14	13	15	15	18
40	40	40	42	42	44	44	46	46
14	14	14	14	14	14	16	16	16
3	3	3	3	3	3	3	3	3
2	3	3	3	3	3	3	3	3
2	2	2	2	3	3	3	3	3
4/14	4/15	4/15	4/15	4/16	4/16	4/17	4/17	4/17
2/14	2/15	2/15	2/15	2/16	2/16	2/17	2/17	2/17
50	52	54	56	59	61	63	65	68
55	57	59	61	64	66	68	70	73
4.5/4	3/6	3/6	3/6	3/6	3.5/6	3.5/6	2.5/6	3.5/6
62	64	67	69	72	74	77	79	82
2.5/12	2.5/12	2/13	2/13	2/13	2.5/13	2/14	2/14	2/14
14	15	15	15	16	16	17	17	17
36	36	38	40	40	40	42	42	42
6/18	6/18	6/18	6/18	5/19	5/20	5/20	5/21	5/22
58	58	60	62	64	66	68	70	72
4/7	4/7	4/7	4/7	4/7	4/7	4/7	4/7	4/7
68	68	70	72	74	76	78	80	82
6/2	6/2	6/2	6/2	6/2	6/2	6/2	6/2	6/2
6	6	5	5	5	6	6	6	6
5	5	5.5	5.5	5.5	6	6	6.5	6.5
2/20	2/20	3/20	3/20	3/20	3/20	3/20	3/20	3/20

Gauge (5 sts x 7.5 rows = 1")

Finished Bust/Chest	30	32	34	36	38	40	42
½ BODY (Back)							
A) CO Straight Body	76	80	86	90	96	100	106
A) CO Cropped Shape Taper	68	72	78	80	86	90	96
B) Inc 1 ea end every ___ rows ___ times	18/4	18/4	20/4	14/5	14/5	14/5	14/5
A) CO Fingertip Taper	84	88	94	100	106	110	116
C) Dec 1 ea end every ___" ___ times	4/4	4/4	4/4	3.5/5	3.5/5	3.5/5	3.5/5
A) CO Long Taper	98	102	108	114	120	124	130
C) Dec 1 ea end every ___" ___ times	2.5/11	2.5/11	2.5/11	2/12	2.5/12	2.5/12	2.5/12
SHAPE ARMHOLE							
Cut In (sleeveless)							
E) BO ___sts beg next ___ rows	4/2	4/2	5/2	5/2	6/2	6/2	7/2
F) Dec 1 ea end EOR ___ times	4	4	5	6	7	7	8
G) Dec 1 ea end every 4th row ___ times	3	4	4	5	6	7	8
Set In							
E) BO ___sts beg next ___ rows	3/2	4/2	4/2	5/2	5/2	5/2	6/2
F) Dec 1 ea end EOR ___ times	4	4	5	6	8	10	11
Modified Drop							
H) BO ___sts beg next 2 rows	3	5	6	8	8	10	10
½ BODY (Pullover Front)							
Boat Neck: (J) BO ctr ___sts	40	40	40	40	42	42	44
Round Neck Shaping							
K) BO ctr ___sts	10	12	12	14	14	14	14
L) BO ___sts ea neck edge 1 time	3	3	3	3	3	3	3
M) BO ___sts ea neck edge 1 time	2	2	2	2	3	3	3
N) Dec 1 ea neck edge EOR ___ times	2	2	2	2	2	2	2
Deep V: Dec ea neck edge							
O) every ___ rows ___ times	4/12	4/13	4/13	4/14	4/15	4/15	4/15
Shallow V: Dec ea neck edge							
O) every ___ rows ___ times	2/12	2/13	2/13	2/14	2/15	2/15	2/15
½ FRONT (Cardigan/Jkt)							
P) CO Straight Shape	38	40	43	45	48	50	53
P) CO Fingertip Taper	42	44	47	50	53	55	58
Q) Dec 1 at side edge every ___" ___ times	4/4	4/4	4/4	3.5/5	3.5/5	3.5/5	3.5/5
P) CO Long Taper	49	51	54	57	60	62	65
Q) Dec 1 at side edge every ___" ___ times	2.5/11	2.5/11	2.5/11	2/12	2.5/12	2.5/12	2.5/12
Round Neck Shaping							
R) BO ___sts beg next 2 rows.	5	6	6	7	7	7	7
Follow shaping (L,M,N) from above							
SLEEVES							
S) CO Long Sleeve	30	30	30	32	34	34	36
T) Inc 1 ea end every ___ rows ___ times	6/17	6/18	6/19	6/19	6/19	6/20	6/20
S) CO Short Sleeve	50	52	54	56	58	60	62
T) Inc 1ea end every ___ rows ___ times	4/7	4/7	4/7	4/7	4/7	4/7	4/7
S) CO Cap Sleeve	60	62	64	66	68	70	72
T) Inc 1ea end every ___ rows ___ times	4/2	4/2	4/2	4/2	6/2	6/2	6/2
CAP SHAPING							
Set In							
U) BO ___sts beg next 2 rows	3	4	4	5	5	5	6
V) Dec 1 ea end EOR for ___"	4	4	4	4.5	4.5	4.5	5
Modified Drop							
W) BO ___sts beg every row ___ times	2/20	2/20	2/22	2/22	2/22	2/22	3/22

44	46	48	50	52	54	56	58	60
110	116	120	156	130	136	140	146	150
100	104	108	114	118	124	128	134	138
16/5	14/6	14/6	14/6	14/6	12/6	12/6	12/6	12/6
120	128	132	138	142	148	152	158	162
3.5/5	3/6	3/6	3/6	3/6	3/6	3/6	3/6	3/6
134	144	148	154	158	164	170	176	180
2.5/12	2.5/14	2/14	2/14	2/14	2/14	2/15	2/15	2/15
4/4	4/4	5/4	5/4	6/4	6/4	7/4	7/4	8/4
9	12	14	17	18	21	20	22	22
8	7	5	4	3	2	2	2	2
6/2	4/4	4/4	5/4	5/4	6/4	6/4	7/4	7/4
12	11	12	12	13	13	14	14	16
12	13	13	13	15	15	17	18	20
44	46	46	48	48	48	50	50	50
16	16	16	16	16	16	18	18	18
3	3	3	3	3	3	3	3	3
3	3	3	3	3	3	3	3	3
2	2	2	3	3	3	3	3	3
4/16	4/16	4/16	3/17	3/17	3/17	3/18	3/18	3/18
2/16	2/16	2/16	2/17	2/17	2/17	2/18	2/18	2/18
55	58	60	63	65	68	70	73	75
60	64	66	69	71	74	76	79	81
3.5/5	3/6	3/6	3/6	3/6	3/6	3/6	3/6	3/6
67	72	74	77	79	82	85	88	90
2.5/12	2.5/14	2/14	2/14	2/14	2/14	2/15	2/15	2/15
8	8	8	8	8	8	9	9	9
38	40	40	42	42	44	44	46	48
6/20	6/20	6/20	6/21	5/22	5/22	5/23	5/23	5/23
64	66	66	68	70	72	74	76	76
4/7	4/7	4/7	4/8	4/8	4/8	4/8	4/8	4/9
74	76	76	78	80	82	84	86	86
6/2	6/2	8/2	6/3	6/3	6/3	6/3	6/3	4/4
6	4	4	5	5	6	6	7	7
5	5	5.5	5.5	5.5	6	6	6.5	6.5
3/22	3/22	3/22	3/22	3/24	3/24	3/24	3/24	3/24

Gauge (5.5 sts x 7.5 rows = 1")

Finished Bust/Chest	30	32	34	36	38	40	42
½ BODY (Back)							
A) CO Straight Body	82	88	94	100	104	110	116
A) CO Cropped Shape Taper	74	80	86	90	94	100	104
B) Inc 1 ea end every ___ rows ___ times	18/4	18/4	20/4	14/5	14/5	14/5	12/6
A) CO Fingertip Taper	90	96	102	110	114	120	128
C) Dec 1 ea end every ___" ___ times	4/4	4/4	4/4	3.5/5	3.5/5	3.5/5	3/6
A) CO Long Taper	106	112	118	126	130	138	144
C) Dec 1 ea end every ___" ___ times	2/12	2/12	2/12	2/13	2/13	2/14	2/14
SHAPE ARMHOLE							
Cut In (sleeveless)							
E) BO ___sts beg next ___ rows	5/2	5/2	6/2	6/2	6/2	6/2	7/2
F) Dec 1 ea end EOR ___ times	3	5	5	6	7	8	10
G) Dec 1 ea end every 4th row ___ times	3	4	4	6	7	8	8
Set In							
E) BO ___sts beg next ___ rows	5/2	5/2	5/2	5/2	5/2	6/2	6/2
F) Dec 1 ea end EOR ___ times	2	3	4	7	8	10	12
Modified Drop							
H) BO ___sts beg next 2 rows	3	5	6	8	8	11	11
½ BODY (Pullover Front)							
Boat Neck: (J) BO ctr ___sts	44	44	44	44	46	46	48
Round Neck Shaping							
K) BO ctr ___sts	12	14	14	14	16	16	18
L) BO ___sts ea neck edge 1 time	3	3	3	3	3	3	3
M) BO ___sts ea neck edge 1 time	2	2	3	3	3	3	3
N) Dec 1 ea neck edge EOR ___ times	2	2	2	2	2	2	2
Deep V: Dec ea neck edge							
O) every ___ rows ___ times	4/13	4/14	4/15	4/15	4/16	4/16	3/17
Shallow V: Dec ea neck edge							
O) every ___ rows ___ times	2/13	2/14	2/15	2/15	2/16	2/16	2/17
½ FRONT (Cardigan/Jkt)							
P) CO Straight Shape	41	44	47	50	52	55	58
P) CO Fingertip Taper	45	48	51	55	57	60	64
Q) Dec 1 at side edge every ___" ___ times	4/4	4/4	4/4	3.5/5	3.5/5	3.5/5	3/6
P) CO Long Taper	53	56	59	63	65	69	72
Q) Dec 1 at side edge every ___" ___ times	2/12	2/12	2/12	2/13	2/13	2/14	2/14
Round Neck Shaping							
R) BO ___sts beg next 2 rows.	6	7	7	7	8	8	9
Follow shaping (L,M,N) from above							
SLEEVES							
S) CO Long Sleeve	30	32	34	36	36	38	40
T) Inc 1 ea end every ___ rows ___ times	5/20	5/20	5/20	5/20	5/21	5/21	5/21
S) CO Short Sleeve	54	56	58	60	62	64	66
T) Inc 1 ea end every ___ rows ___ times	3/8	3/8	3/8	3/8	3/8	3/8	3/8
S) CO Cap Sleeve	64	66	68	70	72	74	76
T) Inc 1 ea end every ___ rows ___ times	3/3	3/3	3/3	3/3	4/3	4/3	4/3
CAP SHAPING							
Set In							
U) BO ___sts beg next 2 rows	5	5	5	5	5	6	6
V) Dec 1 ea end EOR for ___"	4	4	4	4.5	4.5	4.5	5
Modified Drop							
W) BO ____sts beg every row ___ times	2/22	2/22	2/22	2/22	2/22	2/22	2/22

44	46	48	50	52	54	56	58	60
120	126	132	138	142	148	154	160	166
108	112	118	124	128	134	140	146	152
12/6	12/7	12/7	12/7	12/7	12/7	12/7	12/7	12/7
132	140	146	152	156	162	168	174	180
3/6	2.5/7	2.5/7	2.5/7	2.5/7	2.5/7	2.5/7	2.5/7	2.5/7
148	156	162	168	172	180	186	192	198
2/14	2/15	2/15	2/15	2/15	2/16	2/16	2/16	2/16
5/4	5/4	6/4	7/4	7/4	7/4	8/4	8/4	8/4
10	11	15	14	17	20	22	25	27
7	7	5	5	4	3	2	1	1
6/2	4/4	4/4	5/4	5/4	6/4	6/4	7/4	7/4
13	12	14	14	14	14	17	17	19
13	13	14	14	16	16	19	20	23
48	50	50	52	52	54	54	56	56
20	20	20	20	20	20	20	20	20
3	3	3	3	3	3	3	3	3
3	3	3	3	3	3	3	3	3
2	2	2	3	3	3	3	3	3
3/18	3/18	3/18	3/19	3/19	3/19	3/19	4/19	4/19
2/18	2/18	2/18	2/19	2/19	2/19	2/19	2/19	2/19
60	63	66	69	71	74	77	80	83
66	70	73	76	78	81	84	87	90
3/6	2.5/7	2.5/7	2.5/7	2.5/7	2.5/7	2.5/7	2.5/7	2.5/7
74	78	81	84	86	90	93	96	99
2/14	2/15	2/15	2/15	2/15	2/16	2/16	2/16	2/16
10	10	10	10	10	10	10	10	10
42	44	44	46	48	50	50	50	50
5/21	5/21	5/22	5/22	5/22	5/22	5/23	5/24	5/25
68	70	72	76	78	80	82	84	84
3/8	3/8	3/8	4/7	4/7	4/7	4/7	4/7	4/8
78	80	82	84	86	88	88	90	90
4/3	4/3	5/3	5/3	5/3	5/3	5/4	5/4	4/5
6	4	4	5	5	6	6	7	7
5	5	5.5	5.5	5.5	6	6	6.5	6.5
3/22	3/22	3/22	3/22	3/24	3/24	3/24	3/24	3/24

Gauge (6 sts x 8 rows = 1")

Finished Bust/Chest	30	32	34	36	38	40	42
½ BODY (Back)							
A) CO Straight Body	90	96	102	108	114	120	126
A) CO Cropped Shape Taper	82	88	94	96	102	108	114
B) Inc 1 ea end every ___ rows ___ times	20/4	20/4	22/4	14/6	14/6	14/6	14/6
A) CO Fingertip Taper	100	106	112	120	126	132	138
C) Dec 1 ea end every ___" ___ times	3.5/5	3.5/5	3.5/5	3/6	3/6	3/6	3/6
A) CO Long Taper	118	124	130	138	144	150	156
C) Dec 1 ea end every ___" ___ times	2/14	2/14	2/14	1.5/15	1.5/15	1.5/15	1.5/15
SHAPE ARMHOLE							
Cut In (sleeveless)							
E) BO ___ sts beg next ___ rows	4/2	5/2	6/2	7/2	8/2	8/2	9/2
F) Dec 1 ea end EOR ___ times	4	5	5	6	7	8	9
G) Dec 1 ea end every 4th row ___ times	4	5	5	6	7	8	9
Set In							
E) BO ___ sts beg next ___ rows	4/2	5/2	5/2	7/2	8/2	9/2	5/4
F) Dec 1 ea end EOR ___ times	3	4	5	6	7	9	9
Modified Drop							
H) BO ___ sts beg next 2 rows	3	6	6	9	9	12	12
½ BODY (Pullover Front)							
Boat Neck: (J) BO ctr ___ sts	48	48	48	48	50	52	52
Round Neck Shaping							
K) BO ctr ___ sts	14	14	16	18	20	20	22
L) BO ___ sts ea neck edge 1 time	3	3	3	3	3	3	3
M) BO ___ sts ea neck edge 1 time	2	2	2	2	2	2	2
N) Dec 1 ea neck edge EOR ___ times	3	3	3	3	3	3	3
Deep V: Dec ea neck edge							
O) every ___ rows ___ times	4/15	4/15	3/16	3/17	3/18	3/18	3/18
Shallow V: Dec ea neck edge							
O) every ___ rows ___ times	2/15	2/15	2/16	2/17	2/18	2/18	2/18
½ FRONT (Cardigan/Jkt)							
P) CO Straight Shape	45	48	51	54	57	60	63
P) CO Fingertip Taper	50	53	56	60	63	66	69
Q) Dec 1 at side edge every ___" ___ times	3.5/5	3.5/5	3.5/5	3/6	3/6	3/6	3/6
P) CO Long Taper	59	62	65	69	72	75	78
Q) Dec 1 at side edge every ___" ___ times	2/14	2/14	2/14	1.5/15	1.5/15	1.5/15	1.5/15
Round Neck Shaping							
R) BO ___ sts beg next 2 rows.	7	7	8	9	10	10	10
Follow shaping (L,M,N) from above							
SLEEVES							
S) CO Long Sleeve	36	38	40	42	42	44	46
T) Inc 1 ea end every ___ rows ___ times	5/21	5/21	5/21	5/21	5/22	5/22	5/22
S) CO Short Sleeve	60	62	64	66	68	70	72
T) Inc 1ea end every ___ rows ___ times	3/9	3/9	3/9	3/9	3/9	3/9	3/9
S) CO Cap Sleeve	72	74	76	78	80	82	84
T) Inc 1ea end every ___ rows ___ times	3/3	3/3	3/3	3/3	4/3	4/3	4/3
CAP SHAPING							
Set In							
U) BO ___ sts beg next 2 rows	4	5	5	7	8	9	5
V) Dec 1 ea end EOR for ___"	4	4	4	4.5	4.5	4.5	5
Modified Drop							
W) BO ___ sts beg every row ___ times	2/24	2/24	2/24	2/24	3/24	2/24	2/24

44	46	48	50	52	54	56	58	60
132	138	144	150	156	162	168	174	180
120	124	130	136	142	148	154	160	166
14/6	12/7	12/7	12/7	12/7	12/7	12/7	12/7	12/7
144	154	160	166	172	178	184	190	196
3/6	2/8	2/8	2/8	2/8	2/8	2/8	2.5/8	2.5/8
162	172	178	184	190	196	204	210	216
2/15	1.5/17	1.5/17	1.5/17	1.5/17	1.5/17	1.5/18	1.5/18	1.5/18
7/4	7/4	8/4	9/4	7/6	7/6	8/6	9/6	9/6
8	9	9	9	9	10	10	9	11
8	8	9	9	9	9	9	9	10
6/4	6/4	7/4	7/4	7/4	8/4	8/4	9/4	9/4
9	10	10	11	13	12	15	15	18
15	15	15	15	18	18	21	21	24
54	54	54	56	56	58	58	60	60
22	24	24	26	26	26	26	26	26
3	3	3	3	3	3	3	3	3
2	2	2	2	2	2	2	2	2
3	3	3	3	3	3	3	3	3
3/19	3/20	3/20	3/21	3/21	3/21	3/21	3/21	3/21
2/19	2/20	2/20	2/21	2/21	2/21	2/21	2/21	2/21
66	69	72	75	78	81	84	87	90
72	77	80	83	86	89	92	95	98
3/6	2/8	2/8	2/8	2/8	2/8	2/8	2.5/8	2.5/8
81	86	89	92	95	98	102	105	108
2/15	1.5/17	1.5/17	1.5/17	1.5/17	1.5/17	1.5/18	1.5/18	1.5/18
11	12	12	13	13	13	13	13	13
48	50	52	54	54	54	54	54	54
5/23	5/23	5/23	5/23	5/24	5/25	5/26	5/22	5/27
74	76	78	80	82	84	86	88	90
3/10	3/10	4/10	4/10	4/10	4/10	4/10	4/10	4/10
86	88	90	92	94	94	96	96	96
3/4	3/4	3/4	4/4	4/4	3/5	3/5	3/6	3/6
6	6	7	7	7	8	8	9	9
5	5	5.5	5.5	5.5	6	6	6.5	6.5
3/24	3/24	3/24	3/24	3/24	3/24	3/24	3/24	3/24

BY THE SEA, BY THE SEA

SHELLS AND TANKS

Shells and tanks are sleeveless tops that can work on their own or under a jacket. The armholes are higher and the body usually has a close fit. Body styles can range from longer, low-hip length to high-hip, both with straight shaping, or cropped, with a taper from the waist to the armhole for a smoother fit. Armholes can be cut in, revealing shoulders, or set in, for a more traditional style with shoulder coverage. Any neckline option works—the scooped neck will give more of a tank-top feel, while the higher jewel or crew necklines are more conservative. The shallow V or boat neck looks nicely casual. And even though these are warm-weather tops, don't forget the option of a turtle, mock, or funnel neck for a modern look!

SLIP-SLIDING AWAY

DESIGNED BY BARRY KLEIN

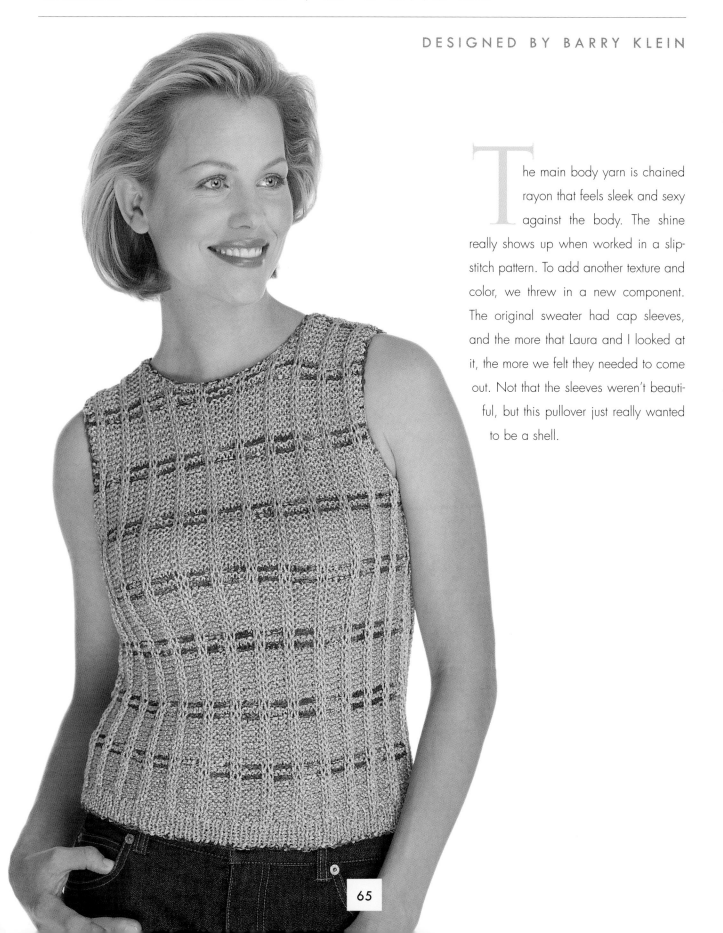

The main body yarn is chained rayon that feels sleek and sexy against the body. The shine really shows up when worked in a slip-stitch pattern. To add another texture and color, we threw in a new component. The original sweater had cap sleeves, and the more that Laura and I looked at it, the more we felt they needed to come out. Not that the sleeves weren't beautiful, but this pullover just really wanted to be a shell.

Style: Sleeveless shell
Length: High hip
Armhole: Set in
Neckline: Jewel neck

Finished Bust Measurement:
36 (40, 44, 48, 52, 56)"

How Do I Vary from the Template?
+ Some stitch counts are adjusted for pattern repeat.
+ Some center neck bind offs are adjusted for odd number of stitches.

Materials

+ 5 (6, 7, 8, 9, 10) skeins Trendsetter Sunshine (50g, 95yds/skein), color 502
+ 2 (2, 2, 2, 2, 2) skeins Trendsetter Binario (25g, 82yds/skein), color 104
+ Size 6 needles
+ Size 7 needles (or size to obtain required gauge)
+ Size F crochet hook

Gauge

5 stitches and 7 rows = 1" in striped slip stitch on size 7 needles

Rib Stitch

(Even number of stitches)

Row 1: *K1, P1; rep from *.
Row 2: Work stitches as they face you.
Rep rows 1 and 2.

Striped Slip Stitch

(Multiple of 7 plus 4)

Row 1: With A, K1, *sl 2 wyib, K5, rep from *, end sl 2 wyib, K1.

Row 2: With A, K1, *P2, K5; rep from *, end P2, K1.

Rows 3–16: Rep rows 1 and 2 seven more times.

Rows 17 and 21: With B, rep row 1.

Rows 18 and 22: With B, K1, *sl 2 wyif, K5; rep from *, end sl 2 wyif, K1.

Rows 19 and 20: With A, rep rows 1 and 2.

Rep rows 1–22.

Back

WITH SIZE 6 needles and Binario, CO loosely 88 (102, 109, 123, 130, 144) sts. Switch to Sunshine and work rib stitch for 1". Switch to size 7 needles and work in striped slip stitch to 13½ (14, 14, 14, 14, 14)" from beg or desired length to underarm. Shape armholes: BO 5 (5, 6, 4, 5, 6) sts at beg of next 2 (2, 2, 4, 4, 4) rows. Dec 1 st at each end EOR 6 (10, 12, 12, 13, 14) times—66 (72, 73, 83, 84, 92) sts. Cont in patt until armhole is 7 (7, 7½, 8, 8, 8½)". BO rem sts.

Front

WORK IN patt as for back until armhole is 4 (4, 4½, 5, 5, 5½)". BO ctr 14 (14, 15, 15, 16, 18) sts. Join new yarn and work both neck edges at same time. BO 3 (3, 3, 3, 3, 3) sts at each neck edge once. BO 2 (3, 3, 3, 3, 3) sts at each neck edge once. Dec 1 st at each neck edge EOR 2 (2, 2, 2, 3, 3) times. Cont in patt until armhole is same length as for back. BO rem sts.

Finishing

Sew shoulder and side seams. With size F crochet hook and Binario, work 1 row of sc and 1 row of slip stitch around neck edge and armhole edges.

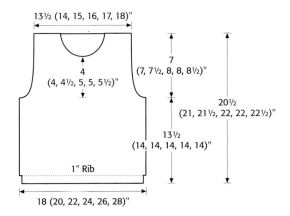

13½ (14, 15, 16, 17, 18)"

4 (4, 4½, 5, 5, 5½)"

7 (7, 7½, 8, 8, 8½)"

20½ (21, 21½, 22, 22, 22½)"

13½ (14, 14, 14, 14, 14)"

1" Rib

18 (20, 22, 24, 26, 28)"

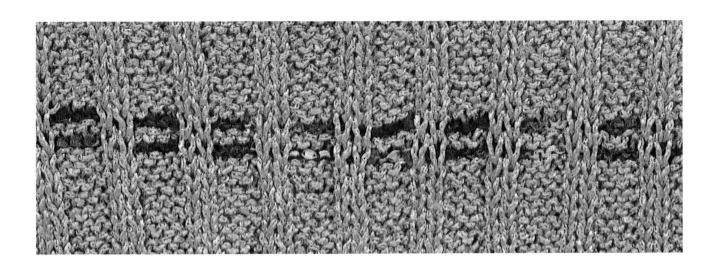

BANANA CABANA

DESIGNED BY BARRY KLEIN

I have always loved this stitch because of the design it creates when the yarn is moved to the front, then wrapped back and around a few stitches. Dolcino, a wide ribbon, is perfect for this because the yarn opens up when it is wrapped. This shell was designed to be long and boxy and is great for all body shapes. It is also perfect if you travel because it folds up small, shakes out easily, and feels great on the body. Once you make one, you'll be making more.

Style: Sleeveless shell
Length: Low hip
Armhole: Set in
Neckline: Jewel neck

Finished Bust Measurement:
36 (40, 44, 48, 52, 56)"

How Do I Vary from the Template?
✦ Stitch count is adjusted for pattern repeat.
✦ Center neck bind off is adjusted for odd number of stitches.

Materials

- 6 (7, 8, 9, 10) skeins Trendsetter Dolcino (50g, 110yds/skein), color 113
- Size 11 needles (or size to obtain required gauge)
- Size H crochet hook

Gauge

4 stitches and 5 rows = 1" in wrap seed stitch

Wrap Seed Stitch
(Multiple of 6 plus 5)

Wrap 3 = <Wyib, sl 3 sts to right needle. Move yarn to front and slip same 3 sts back to left needle.> Work <> 2 times total; wyib, sl 3 sts to right needle and continue.

Rows 1 and 9: K1 (3, 1, 1, 3, 1), *sl 1 wyib, P1; rep from *, end sl 1 wyib, K1 (3, 1, 1, 3, 1).

Rows 2, 4, 6, 8, 10: K1 (3, 1, 1, 3, 1), purl to last 1 (3, 1, 1, 3, 1) sts, K1 (3, 1, 1, 3, 1).

Rows 3 and 7: K1 (3, 1, 1, 3, 1), *P1, sl 1 wyib; rep from *, end P1, K1 (3, 1, 1, 3, 1).

Row 5: K1 (3, 1, 1, 3, 1), *wrap 3, P1, sl 1 wyib, P1; rep from *, end wrap 3, K1 (3, 1, 1, 3, 1).

Row 11: K1 (3, 1, 1, 3, 1), *P1, sl 1 wyib, P1, wrap 3; rep from *, end P1, sl 1 wyib, P1, K1 (3, 1, 1, 3, 1).

Row 12: K1 (3, 1, 1, 3, 1), purl to last 1 (3, 1, 1, 3, 1) sts, K1 (3, 1, 1, 3, 1).

Rep rows 1-12.

Back

CO 71 (83, 89, 95, 106, 113) sts. Work in wrap seed stitch to 15 (15½, 15½, 15½, 15½, 15½)" from beg or desired length to underarm. Shape armholes: BO 4 (5, 6, 4, 5, 6) sts at beg of next 2 (2, 2, 4, 4, 4) rows. Dec 1 st at each end EOR 5 (7, 8, 8, 8, 9) times—53 (59, 61, 63, 70, 71) sts. Cont in patt until armhole is 6½ (6½, 7, 7½, 7½, 8)" from beg. BO ctr 19 (21, 21, 23, 22, 23) sts. Join new yarn and work both neck edges at same time. Cont in patt until armhole is 7½ (7½, 8, 8½, 8½, 9)". BO rem sts.

Front

Work in patt as for back until armhole is 4 (4, 4½, 5, 5, 5½)" from beg. BO ctr 9 (11, 11, 13, 12, 13) sts. Join new yarn and work both neck edges at same time. At neck edge, BO 3 sts once, then BO 2 sts once. Dec 1 st at each neck edge EOR 2 (2, 2, 2, 3, 3) times. Cont in patt until armhole is same length as for back. BO rem sts.

Finishing

Sew left shoulder seam. Pick up 71 (71, 71, 77, 77, 77) sts around neck edge. Work rows 1–4 of wrap seed stitch for 1½". BO in patt. Sew right shoulder seam. Sew side seams. With size H crochet hook and Dolcino, work 1 row of sc and 1 row of slip stitch around armhole openings.

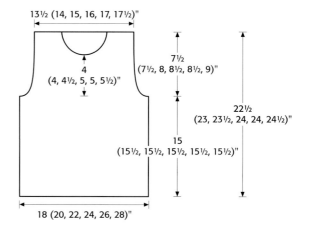

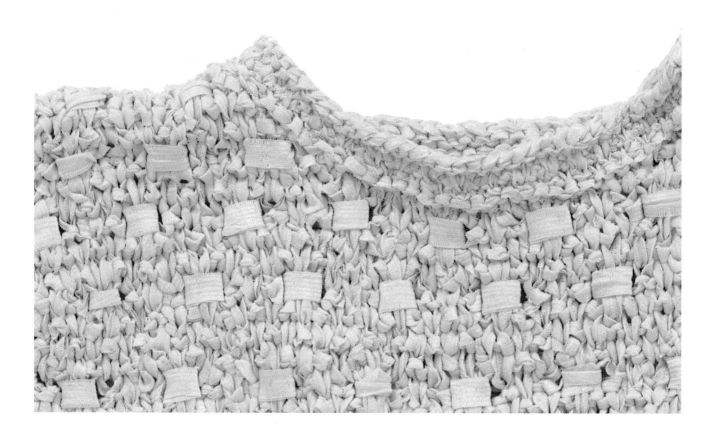

FAN DANCE

DESIGNED BY LAURA BRYANT

Two of my favorite novelty yarns—velvety soft chenille and fabulous feathery Fern! What could be more inviting? To tame the chenille, I worked it as a double strand on smaller needles. A simple tapered shape with cut-in armholes directs attention to the neckline trim. What fun!

Style: Sleeveless tank

Length: Cropped

Taper: Narrower hem to wider bust

Armhole: Cut in

Neckline: Modified scoop on front and back with wide band

Finished Bust Measurement:

34 (38, 42, 46, 50)"

How Do I Vary from the Template?

✦ Neck depths are adjusted to accommodate the large band.

✦ Back neck is somewhat higher than front for proper tank-style fit.

Materials

✦ 14 (15, 17, 20, 24) skeins Prism Maribu (1 oz, 55yds/skein), color Lipstick

✦ 1 (1, 1, 1, 1) skein Prism Fern (2 oz, 58yds/skein), color Lipstick

✦ Size 6 needles (or size to obtain required gauge)

✦ Size 9 needles

✦ Size F crochet hook

Gauge

4 stitches and 6 rows = 1" in stockinette stitch on size 6 needles with 2 strands Maribu held together

Back

WITH SIZE 6 needles and 2 strands Maribu held together, CO 62 (68, 76, 82, 90) sts. Work 6 rows garter st, then switch to St st, inc 1 st at each edge every 20 (14, 14, 12, 12) rows 3 (4, 4, 5, 5) times—68 (76, 84, 92, 100) sts. Work to 12 (12, 11½, 12, 12)" from beg or desired length to underarm. Shape armholes: BO 4 (5, 6, 7, 4) sts at beg of next

2 (2, 2, 2, 4) rows. Dec 1 st at each edge EOR 4 (5, 6, 7, 8) times. BO 1 st at each edge every 4 rows 3 (5, 6, 7, 8) times—46 (46, 48, 50, 52) sts. Work to 15½ (16½, 17½, 18½, 19)" from beg. Shape neck: BO ctr 8 (10, 10, 12, 12) sts. Attach 2nd ball of yarn and work both sides at once: At each neck edge, BO 3 sts once, then 2 sts once. Dec 1 st at each neck edge EOR 2 times. Work until back is 18½ (19, 19, 19½, 20)" from beg. BO rem sts.

Front

WORK AS for back to 13 (13, 14, 15, 15½)", then shape neck as for back.

Finishing

SEW LEFT shoulder seam. With Fern and size 9 needles, pick up 30 (30, 32, 34, 34) sts along back neck and 56 (60, 62, 64, 66) sts along front neck

for a total of 86 (90, 94, 98, 100) sts. Knit 5 rows; on next row, knit and dec 4 sts total, 2 front and 2 back, in the area of the neck curve. Knit 2 more rows, then with WS facing, BO all sts firmly. Sew other shoulder seam. Sew side seams. With size F crochet hook and 2 strands Maribu, work 1 row sc and 1 row rev sc around each armhole edge.

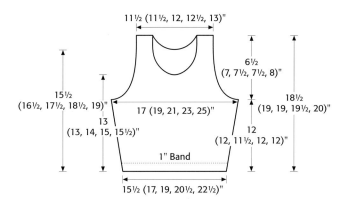

Schematic measurements:
- 11½ (11½, 12, 12½, 13)"
- 6½ (7, 7½, 7½, 8)"
- 15½ (16½, 17½, 18½, 19)"
- 18½ (19, 19, 19½, 20)"
- 17 (19, 21, 23, 25)"
- 13 (13, 14, 15, 15½)"
- 12 (12, 11½, 12, 12)"
- 1" Band
- 15½ (17, 19, 20½, 22½)"

PULL ONE OVER

Traditional pullovers provide the knitter with a perfect blank canvas on which to create. Body styles range from high hip to low, with straight shaping; to fingertip, either tapered or straight. The simple shape makes it easy to use fancy stitches or color work. The option of set-in or modified-drop armholes allows adaptation for dressy or casual styles. Sleeves can be the traditional long or abbreviated to short or cap sleeves. Short sleeves, starting just above the elbow, provide a bit more coverage than cap sleeves, which are a nice alternative to sleeveless and come just below the armhole opening.

74

OCEANS AND AQUAS

DESIGNED BY BARRY KLEIN AND FAYLA REISS

This sweater is a prime example of what knitting "freedom" is all about. I worked on this design with my friend Fayla Reiss, who is the queen of letting it all happen. I made a sketch of what I wanted, set the yarns down, and told Fayla, "Have fun. I want lots of different stripes and lots of play with colors." Here you have the results, a truly fun sweater that has stripes in every sequence possible. The two-piece front can also be left open, making this wonderful pullover into a cardigan. Because of the linear stripes, we made a square neckline by binding off all the necessary stitches at the point where we were to shape the normal crew neck. We used the template for the numbers and made the changes we wanted. The book really works!

Style: Pullover

Length: Low hip

Sleeves: Long, with modified-drop armhole shaping and flat sleeve bind-off

Neckline: Square neck bind-off at crew-neck height

Finished Bust Measurement:
36 (40, 44, 48, 52, 56)"

How Do I Vary from the Template?

+ Fronts are knit in two pieces and seamed together with opening at top and bottom.
+ Neckline is modified to straight bind off, producing a square neckline.
+ There is no sleeve cap shaping to accommodate stripe pattern, so sleeve is wider at top so that straight bind off fits into armhole properly. Width must match armhole depth times two.
+ The shoulders are bound off in steps to provide a more tailored fit.

Materials

+ (A)   2 (3, 3, 3, 3, 4) skeins Trendsetter Sunshine (50g, 95yds/skein), color 31
+ (B)   2 (3, 3, 3, 3, 4) skeins Trendsetter Sunshine, color 53
+ (C)   2 (3, 3, 3, 3, 4) skeins Trendsetter Sunshine, color 06
+ (D)   3 (3, 3, 3, 4, 4) skeins Trendsetter Charm (20g, 90yds/skein), color 60
+ Size 6 needles (or size to obtain required gauge)
+ Size F crochet hook

Gauge

5 stitches and 7 rows = 1" in stockinette stitch

Back

WITH SIZE 6 needles and C, CO 90 (100, 110, 120, 130, 140) sts. Work in St st in following stripe sequence: *4 rows A, 4 rows B, 4 rows C*. Rep from * to * for entire back. Work to 14½ (15, 15, 15, 15, 15)" from beg or desired length to underarm. Shape armholes: BO 8 (10, 12, 13, 15, 17) sts at beg of next 2 rows—74 (80, 86, 94, 100, 106) sts. Cont until armhole is 7½ (7½, 8, 8½, 8½, 9)" from beg. BO 8 (9, 9, 11, 11, 12) sts at beg of next 2 rows. BO 8 (8, 9, 10, 11, 12) sts at beg of next 2 rows. BO 7 (8, 9, 10, 11, 12) sts at beg of next 2 rows. BO rem sts.

Right Front

WITH SIZE 6 needles and C, CO 45 (50, 55, 60, 65, 70) sts. Work right front stripe sequence (below) in St st. Rep from beg for any balance of stripes necessary for differences in row gauge. At same time, when 14½ (15, 15, 15, 15, 15)" from beg or same length as back to underarm, shape armhole: BO 8 (10, 12, 13, 15, 17) sts at armhole edge once. Cont until armhole is 5 (5, 5½, 6, 6, 6½)". BO 14 (15, 16, 16, 17, 17) sts at neck edge once. Cont until armhole is same length as back to shoulder shaping. BO 8 (9, 9, 11, 11, 12) sts at armhole edge once. BO 8 (8, 9, 10, 11, 12) sts at armhole edge once. BO rem sts.

Right Front Stripe Sequence

4 rows C
4 rows B
4 rows A
24 rows D
4 rows A
4 rows B
8 rows C
4 rows B
4 rows A
10 rows D
4 rows A
4 rows B
4 rows C
4 rows A
4 rows B
4 rows C
10 rows D
4 rows C
4 rows B
4 rows A
10 rows D
4 rows A
4 rows B
4 rows C
8 rows A
4 rows B
4 rows C

Left Front

WITH SIZE 6 needles and C, CO 45 (50, 55, 60, 65, 70) sts. Work left front stripe sequence (below) in St st. Rep stripes from beg for any difference in row gauge. At same time, when 14½ (15, 15, 15, 15)" from beg or same length as other front, BO 8 (10, 12, 13, 15, 17) sts at arm edge once. Cont until armhole is same length as right front up to neck shaping. BO 14 (15, 16, 16, 17, 17) sts at neck edge once. Cont until armhole is same length as right front up to shoulder shaping. BO 8 (9, 9, 11, 11, 12) sts at arm edge once. BO 8 (8, 9, 10, 11, 12) sts at arm edge once. BO rem sts.

Left Front Stripe Sequence

4 rows A
4 rows B
4 rows C

10 rows D
4 rows C
4 rows B
4 rows A
24 rows D
4 rows A
4 rows B
6 rows C
4 rows B
4 rows A
10 rows D
4 rows A
4 rows B
4 rows C
4 rows A
4 rows B
4 rows C
10 rows D
4 rows C
4 rows B
4 rows A
6 rows D
4 rows A
4 rows B
4 rows C

Sleeves

WITH SIZE 6 needles and B, CO 36 (36, 40, 40, 46, 46) sts. Work following stripe patt in St st: *2 rows A, 4 rows B, 4 rows C, 12 rows D, rep from * 2 times total; then **4 rows C, 4 rows B, 2 rows A, 12 rows D, rep from ** for balance of sleeve. Work in stripes, inc 1 st at each end every 6 (6, 6, 5, 6, 6) rows 20 (20, 20, 23, 20, 22) times—76 (76, 80, 86, 86, 90) sts. Work to 20 (20½, 21½, 22, 22½, 23)" from beg. BO rem sts evenly.

Finishing

SEW SHOULDER seams. Set sleeves into armhole edge. Sew rem underarm and side seams.

For a closed front, mark 2" down on each front piece at top and bottom. Sew fronts together from marker to marker. With size F crochet hook and A, work 1 row sc around entire neck edge. Then work 1 row of slip stitch into front loop of sc on previous row around entire neck edge. With size F crochet hook and C, work 1 row of slip stitch into front half of cast-on stitch along bottom edge. With size F crochet hook and B, work 1 row of slip stitch into front half of sleeve cast-on stitch to finish off. If you want to make a cardigan, leave fronts open and work the neck crochet around the neck edge and front edges, adding buttonholes if desired.

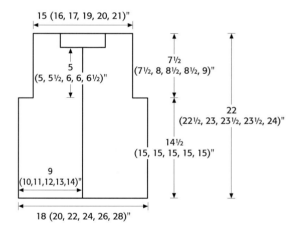

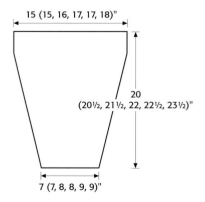

TOP THIS ONE

DESIGNED BY LAURA BRYANT

This fun, striped summer top takes advantage of three multicolored yarns of different textures. Because the yarns are so interesting, stockinette is all that is needed. Simple garter bands and a crocheted edge at the neck provide finishing touches.

Style: Pullover
Length: High hip
Sleeves: Cap with set-in armhole shaping
Neckline: Jewel neck

Finished Bust Measurement:
36 (40, 44, 48, 52)"

How Do I Vary from the Template?
✦   No variation

Materials

- (A)   5 (6, 7, 8, 9) skeins Prism Diana
  (2 oz, 55yds/skein), color Harvest
- (B)   2 (2, 2, 3, 3) skeins Prism Tubino
  (2 oz, 165yds/skein), color Harvest
- (C)   3 (4, 5, 6, 6) skeins Prism Cotton
  Crepe (2 oz, 75yds/skein), color Candy Apple
- Size 10 needles
- Size 11 needles (or size to obtain required
  gauge)
- Size J crochet hook

Gauge

3½ stitches and 5 rows = 1" in stockinette stitch on
size 11 needles

NOTE: One-row stripe pattern: Cast on with A, drop A
and attach B, work across with B, drop B, attach C,
work across with C, and A is waiting at the other end.
Repeat A, B, and C sequence throughout.

Back

WITH SIZE 10 needles, CO 64 (70, 78, 84, 92) sts.
Work 4 rows garter st in stripe sequence. Switch to
size 11 needles and work one-row stripe patt in St
st to 13 (13½, 13½, 13½, 13½)" from beg or
desired length to underarm. Shape armholes: BO 4
(5, 5, 5, 3) sts at beg of next 2 (2, 2, 2, 4) rows, dec
1 st at each edge EOR 4 (5, 8, 9, 10) times—48
(50, 52, 56, 60) sts. Work even to armhole depth of
7½ (7½, 8, 8½, 8½)". BO rem sts.

Front

WORK AS for back to 4 (4, 4½, 5, 5)" from beg of armhole shaping. Cont to work armhole shaping as for back. Shape neck: BO ctr 10 (10, 10, 10, 12) sts. Attach 2nd ball of yarn and work both neck edges at same time: At each neck edge, BO 2 (3, 3, 3, 3) sts once, then BO 2 sts once. Dec 1 st at each neck edge once. When same length as back, BO rem sts.

Sleeves

WITH SIZE 10 needles, CO 46 (48, 50, 52, 56) sts. Work garter st in stripe sequence for 4 rows. Switch to size 11 needles and work St st, inc 1 st at each edge every 3 (4, 4, 5, 5) rows 2 times—50 (52, 54, 56, 60) sts. Work to 1½ (2, 2, 2½, 2½)" from beg or desired length to underarm. Shape cap: BO 4 (5, 5, 5, 3) sts at beg of next 2 rows. Dec 1 st at each edge EOR to cap depth of 4½ (4½, 5, 5½, 5½)". BO rem sts.

Finishing

SEW SHOULDER seams. Sew side and sleeve seams. Set sleeves into armhole edge. With size J crochet hook, work 1 rnd sc and 1 rnd rev sc around neck edge.

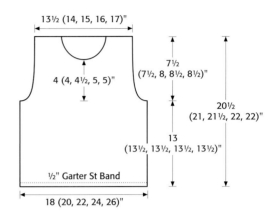

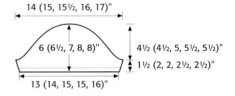

ADOBE DREAMS

DESIGNED BY LAURA BRYANT

Three striking yarns, a bit of glimmer, and an abbreviated style—what better dream is there? This great topper is exactly the kind of sweater I love to wear. The cropped, tapered shape looks great with slim skirts and tailored pants. Flecks of gold allow you to dress up or down, and the neat rolled neckline is flattering yet not constricting. A simple diagonal variation of the half linen stitch mixes the colors beautifully.

Style:	Pullover
Length:	Cropped
Taper:	Narrower hem to wider bust
Sleeves:	Short with modified-drop armhole shaping
Neckline:	Crew with rolled neck

Finished Bust Measurement:
36 (40, 44, 48, 52)"

How Do I Vary from the Template?
✦ Stitch count is adjusted for pattern repeat.

Materials

✦ (A) 2 (3, 3, 4, 4) skeins Prism Star (2oz, 135yds/skein), color Harvest
✦ (B) 2 (3, 3, 4, 4) skeins Prism Flash (2oz, 125yds/skein), color Sagebrush
✦ (C) 3 (3, 4, 4, 5) skeins Prism Pearls (2oz, 105yds/skein), color Terra Cotta
✦ Size 9 straight needles (or size to obtain required gauge)
✦ Size 9 circular needle (16")

Gauge

4½ stitches and 8½ rows = 1" in diagonal slip stitch

Diagonal Slip Stitch
(Multiple of 4 plus 2)

NOTE: Patt is worked with 1 row of each yarn. Cast on with A, drop A and attach B, work across with B, drop B, attach C, work across with C, and A is waiting at the other end.

Row 1: K1, *K3, sl 1 wyif; rep from *, end K1.
Row 2: P4, *sl 1 wyib, P3; rep from *, end slip 1 wyib, P1.
Row 3: K2, *sl 1 wyif, K3; rep from *, end slip 1 wyif, K3.
Row 4: P2, *sl 1 wyib, P3; rep from *.
Rep rows 1–4.

Back

WITH A, CO 72 (80, 90, 98, 108) sts. Work diagonal slip stitch in stripe sequence, inc 1 st at each edge every 14 rows 5 times—82 (90, 100, 108, 118) sts. Work to 10½ (11, 11, 11, 11)" from beg or desired length to underarm. Shape armholes: BO 7 (9, 11, 11, 14) sts at beg of next 2 rows—68 (72, 78, 86, 90) sts. Cont in patt to 18½ (19, 19½, 20, 20)" from beg. BO all sts firmly.

Front

WORK IN patt and stripe sequence as for back to 15 (15½, 16, 16½, 17)". Shape neck: Place ctr 12 (12, 14, 14, 14) sts on holder. Attach 2nd ball of yarn and work both sides at once: At each neck edge, BO 3 sts once, BO 2 (2, 2, 3, 3) sts once. Dec 1 st at each neck edge EOR 1 (2, 2, 2, 3) times. When same length as back, BO all sts firmly.

Sleeves

WITH A, CO 50 (54, 58, 62, 66) sts. Work in patt and stripe sequence as for body, inc 1 st at each edge every 4 rows 7 times—64 (68, 72, 76, 80) sts. When sleeve is 5½ (6, 6½, 7, 7)" long or desired length to shoulder less 3", shape cap: BO 2 (2, 2, 3, 3) sts at beg of next 20 rows. BO rem sts.

Finishing

SEW SHOULDER seams. Sew sleeve cap into armhole edge between the bound-off sts. Sew side and sleeve seams, tacking sleeve edge to bound-off sts at armhole.

Collar

With 16" circular needle and next yarn in rotation for ctr front sts, beg at left shoulder seam and pick up 12 (12, 14, 14, 14) sts along side neck edge, 12 (12, 14, 14, 14) sts from st holder, 12 (12, 14, 14, 14) sts to next shoulder seam, and 24 (24, 26, 26, 26) sts along back neck. Work in patt, moving sl st 1 st to left every rnd. Work for 3", then BO all sts very loosely.

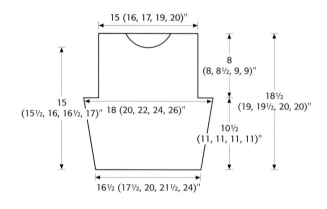

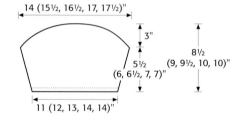

PIN BOX PASSION

DESIGNED BY LAURA BRYANT

I have had a passion for mosaic stitches for many years. Even the most complicated of them are remarkably easy to knit, since each row is worked with only one color, working some stitches and slipping others. The pin box pattern is a delightful maze of boxes within boxes, made more magical by the use of two different hand-dyed yarns. The simple, straight shape, with a modified-drop sleeve and crew neck, make this a true unisex style. As large or as small as you wish to go, the only watch point is the large repeat, which means sizing is limited in its fine-tuning. So, find your desired measurement, then pick the closest size. If in doubt, go larger!

Style: Pullover

Length: Slightly shorter than fingertip

Sleeves: Long, with modified-drop armhole shaping

Neckline: Crew neck with ribbed band

Finished Bust/Chest Measurement (Unisex):
36 (44, 48, 54, 60)"

How Do I Vary from the Template?

✦ The large pattern repeat requires major adjustments in stitch count, which leads to sizing compromises.

✦ Cast on stitches are reduced for rib border; stitches are increased to get as close to template numbers as the pattern repeat allows on the first row of the pattern.

✦ The neck, armhole shaping, and sleeve cap shaping are adjusted to accommodate the pattern repeat.

Materials

✦ (A) 5 (6, 7, 8, 9) skeins Prism Andee (2 oz, 114yds/skein), color Peacock

✦ (B) 4 (5, 6, 7, 8) skeins Prism Andee (2 oz, 114yds/skein), color Harvest

✦ Size 6 straight needles

✦ Size 6 circular needle (16")

✦ Size 9 straight needles (or size to obtain required gauge)

Gauge

4 stitches and 7 rows = 1" in pin box pattern on size 9 needles

Rib Stitch

(Even number of stitches)

Row 1: *K1, P1; rep from *.
Row 2: *K1, P1; rep from *.
Rep rows 1 and 2.

Pin Box Pattern

(Multiple of 12 plus 3)

NOTE: On all odd-numbered (RS) rows, slip all sl sts wyib.

Row 1: With A, knit.
Row 2: With A, purl.
Row 3: With B, K1, *sl 1, K11; rep from *, end sl 1, K1.
Row 4 and all even-numbered (WS) rows: Purl all sts knitted on previous row, and slip all the same slipped sts wyif.
Row 5: With A, K2, *sl 1, K9, sl 1, K1; rep from *, end K1.
Row 7: With B, (K1, sl 1) twice, *K7, (sl 1, K1) twice, sl 1; rep from *, end K7, (sl 1, K1) twice.
Row 9: With A, K2, sl 1, K1, sl 1, *K5, (sl 1, K1) 3 times, sl 1; rep from *, end K5, sl 1, K1, sl 1, K2.
Row 11: With B, (K1, sl 1) 3 times, *K3, (sl 1, K1) 4 times, sl 1; rep from *, end K3, (sl 1, K1) 3 times.
Row 13: With A, K2, *sl 1, K1; rep from *, end K1.
Rows 15, 17, 19, 21, 23, 25: Rep rows 11, 9, 7, 5, 3, 1 in order.
Row 27: With B, K7, *sl 1, K11; rep from *, end last rep K7.
Row 29: With A, K6, *sl 1, K1, sl 1, K9; rep from *, end last rep K6.
Row 31: With B, K5, *(sl 1, K1) twice, sl 1, K7; rep from *, end last rep K5.

Alternate colorway: Orchard and Aspen

Row 33: With A, K4, *(sl 1, K1) 3 times, sl 1, K5; rep from *, end last rep K4.
Row 35: With B, K3, *(sl 1, K1) 4 times, sl 1, K3; rep from *.
Row 37: With A, rep row 13.
Rows 39, 41, 43, 45, 47: Rep rows 35, 33, 31, 29, 27 in order.
Row 48: See row 4.
Rep rows 1–48.

Back

WITH SIZE 6 needles and A, CO 54 (76, 88, 100, 112) sts. Work in rib stitch for 2½", then switch to size 9 needles and inc 9 (11, 11, 11, 11) sts evenly across row 1 of pin box pattern—63 (87, 99, 111, 123) sts. Work in pin box pattern for 2 (2½, 2½, 3, 3) repeats, approx 14½ (17½, 17½, 21, 21)" from beg. Shape armholes: BO 0 (12, 12, 12, 12) sts at beg of next 2 rows—63 (63, 75, 87, 99) sts. Cont in patt as established for 1½ more repeats (ending on row 24 or 48 of patt), approx 23½ (26½, 26½, 30, 30)" from beg. BO rem sts firmly.

Front

WORK IN patt as for back to 21 (24, 24, 27½, 27½)". Shape neck: BO ctr 17 sts, then working each side separately, BO at each neck edge 3 sts once, 2 sts once, then dec 1 st at each neck edge EOR 2 times. When same length as back, BO rem sts firmly.

Sleeves

WITH SIZE 6 needles and A, CO 33 (35, 37, 39, 41) sts. Work in rib stitch for 2½". Switch to size 9 needles and inc 6 (16, 14, 12, 10) sts evenly across first row of pin box pattern—39 (51, 51, 51, 51) sts. Work in pin box pattern, inc 1 st at each edge every 8 rows 10 times, working new sts into patt (it may be helpful to place a marker between new sts and established patt for counting ease)—59 (71, 71, 71, 71) sts. When 2 (2½, 2½, 2½, 2½) repeats are completed, approx 17 (21, 21, 21, 21)" from beg, shape cap: BO 3 sts at beg of next 20 rows. BO rem sts.

Finishing

SEW SHOULDER seams. Sew sleeves to armhole edge between bound-off sts. Sew side and sleeve seams, tacking sleeve edge to bound-off sts of armhole. For neckband, with 16" circular needle, pick up 78 sts around neck edge. Work in rib stitch for 1". BO loosely in rib.

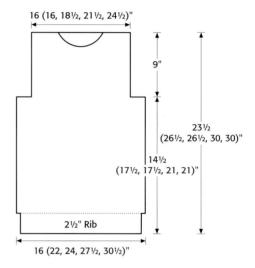

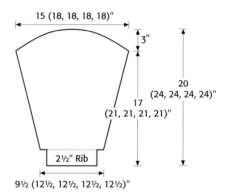

ARROYO AVENUE

DESIGNED BY LAURA BRYANT

Big ribs equal big elasticity, so the gauge for this sweater was figured on a swatch that was in a slightly stretched state, rather than relaxed. This mimics how the sweater will sit on the body. The more the swatch is stretched while measuring, the tighter the fit will be. For a truly draped sweater, take a gauge over a completely relaxed swatch. The color-coordinated but texturally different yarns create a pleasing harmony. Garter-stitch rows are added to reduce the cling and to pop the textured yarns more.

Style: Pullover

Length: Cropped

Sleeves: Long, with set-in armhole shaping

Neckline: Boat neck with loose funnel that rolls down

Finished Bust Measurement:

36 (40, 44, 48, 52)" slightly stretched; approx 26 (30, 34, 38, 42)" unstretched

How Do I Vary from the Template?

+ Stitch counts are adjusted for pattern repeat, both in body and at neck shaping.
+ Shoulder width is a compromise between relaxed and stretched gauge (more stitches are removed than the template would indicate).
+ Cap shaping is adjusted for rib.
+ Sleeves are a bit longer because of rib.

Materials

+ 6 (7, 8, 9, 10) skeins Prism Matte (1.5 oz, 115yds/skein), color Arroyo
+ 2 (2, 3, 3, 4) skeins Prism Cleo (1.5 oz, 82yds/skein), color Arroyo
+ 5 (6, 7, 8, 8) skeins Prism Dazzle (1 oz, 116yds/skein), color Arroyo
+ 12 (13, 14, 16, 18) skeins Prism Sunshine (1 oz, 65yds/skein), color Arroyo
+ Size 6 straight needles (or size to obtain required gauge)
+ Size 6 circular needle (16")

Gauge

6 sts and 8 rows = 1" in large rib stitch and stripe sequence, measured slightly stretched

Large Rib Stitch

(Multiple of 6 plus 2)

Worked on all Matte rows only

Row 1: K1, *K3, P3; rep from*, end K1.
Row 2: P1, *K3, P3; rep from*, end P1.

Stripe Sequence

NOTE: The stripe sequence not only alternates yarns, but also stitches.

4 rows Matte rib
2 rows Sunshine garter
4 rows Matte rib
2 rows Cleo garter
4 rows Matte rib
2 rows Sunshine garter
4 rows Matte rib
2 rows Dazzle garter

Back

WITH MATTE, CO 110 (122, 134, 146, 158) sts. Work in large rib stitch and stripe sequence to 11 (11½, 11½, 11½, 11½)" or desired length to underarm. Measure by holding piece upright and stretched slightly along needle to mimic how it will sit on body, remembering that sideways stretch causes length to pull up. Shape armholes: BO 7 (9, 6, 7, 7) sts at beg of next 2 (2, 4, 4, 4) rows. Dec 1 st at each edge EOR 6 (9, 9, 10, 13) times—84 (86, 92, 98, 104) sts. Work to 18½ (19, 19½, 20, 20)" from beg. BO rem sts firmly.

Front

WORK IN patt and stripe sequence as for back to shoulder. BO 16 (17, 20, 23, 26) sts, place ctr 52 sts on holder, and BO rem 16 (17, 20, 23, 26) sts.

Sleeves

WITH MATTE, CO 42 (42, 50, 50, 56) sts. Work in patt and stripe sequence as for body, inc 1 st at each edge every 5 rows 21 (22, 23, 23, 24) times—84 (86, 96, 96, 104) sts. When sleeve is 15½ (16, 16½, 16½, 17)" from beg or desired length to underarm (remembering that as the rib stretches out around the arm, it will shorten), shape cap: BO 7 (9, 6, 7, 7) sts at beg of next 2 rows. Dec 1 st at each edge every row to a cap depth of 4½ (4½, 5, 5½, 5½)". BO rem sts, working every 2nd and 3rd sts together as you bind off (this helps to ease fullness into cap top).

Finishing

SEW SHOULDER, side, and sleeve seams. Set sleeves into armhole edges. With circular needle, pick up 52 sts from holder and 52 sts along back neck. Working in rib stitch and stripe sequence, on first row, dec 1 st at each shoulder seam to keep patt intact so there are 102 sts. Work in patt for 4". BO rem sts loosely in patt.

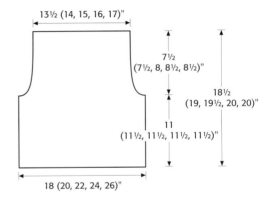

13½ (14, 15, 16, 17)"

7½
(7½, 8, 8½, 8½)"

18½
(19, 19½, 20, 20)"

11
(11½, 11½, 11½, 11½)"

18 (20, 22, 24, 26)"

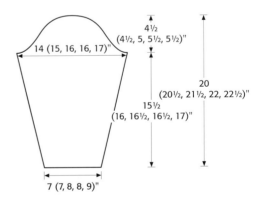

4½
(4½, 5, 5½, 5½)"

14 (15, 16, 16, 17)"

20
(20½, 21½, 22, 22½)"

15½
(16, 16½, 16½, 17)"

7 (7, 8, 8, 9)"

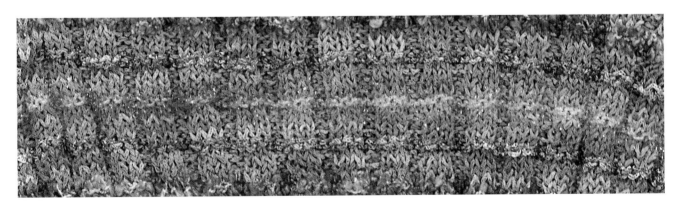

JUNGLE JUMPER

DESIGNED BY BARRY KLEIN

This sweater was designed to show the play of color and texture. Both yarns are dyed in the same colorway, so when stripes of garter stitch and ribbing are alternated, the stripes become less important and the textures blend more. The design has a modified-drop armhole, but I chose to make the sleeve top bind off straight to avoid layered stripes at the top of the sleeve. I love playing with collars and so I wanted something different here. The off-center collar adds another dimension but can be sewn up to create a regular rolled collar if desired.

Style: Pullover
Length: Low hip
Sleeves: Long, with modified-drop armhole shaping and straight bind-off
Neckline: Crew neck with off-center collar

Finished Bust Measurement:
34 (38, 42, 46, 50, 54, 58)"

How Do I Vary from the Template?

+ Stitch counts are adjusted for pattern repeat.
+ Sleeves have more stitches initially to accommodate pattern repeat, so increases are fewer. There is no sleeve cap shaping to accommodate the pattern. Sleeve is wider at top so that straight bind off fits into armhole properly.

Materials

+ 4 (5, 5, 6, 6, 7, 7) skeins Trendsetter Marbella (50g/93yds/skein), color 4199
+ 4 (5, 6, 7, 8, 8, 9) skeins Trendsetter Vintage (50g/95yds/skein), color 4379
+ Size 7 needles
+ Size 8 needles (or size required to obtain gauge)
+ Size 9 needles

Gauge

4 stitches and 6 rows = 1" in garter stitch or large rib stitch slightly stretched on size 9 needles

Large Rib Stitch
(Multiple of 6 plus extra, depending on size)

Row 1: *K3, P3; rep from *, end K3 (3, 0, 3, 3, 0, 3).
Row 2: P3 (3, 0, 3, 3, 0, 3), *K3, P3; rep from *.
Rep rows 1 and 2.

Back

WITH SIZE 7 needles and Marbella, CO 69 (75, 84, 93, 99, 108, 117) sts. Work in garter st for 5 rows. Switch to size 8 needles and work in following stripe sequence to 15 (15, 14½, 15, 15, 15, 15)" from beg or desired length to underarm: 6 rows Vintage in large rib stitch, 6 rows Marbella in garter st. Shape armholes: BO 4 (6, 8, 10, 10, 12, 14) sts at beg of next 2 rows—61 (63, 68, 73, 79, 84, 89) sts. Cont in patt as established until armhole is 7½ (8, 8½, 8½, 9, 9½, 10)". BO rem sts in patt.

Front

WORK IN patt as for back until armhole is 4½ (5, 5½, 5½, 6, 6½, 7)". BO ctr 9 (9, 10, 11, 11, 12, 13) sts. Attach 2nd ball of yarn and work both sides of neck at same time: At each neck edge, BO 3 sts once, then BO 2 sts once. Dec 1 st at each neck edge EOR 2 (2, 2, 2, 2, 3, 3) times. Cont until front is same length as back. BO rem sts in patt.

Sleeves

WITH SIZE 7 needles and Marbella, CO 30 (30, 30, 33, 33, 33, 36) sts. Work in garter st for 5 rows. Switch to size 8 needles and stripe sequence as for body, inc 1 st at each end every 6 (5, 5, 5, 5, 5, 5) rows 15 (17, 19, 18, 20, 22, 22) times, working new sts into patt—60 (64, 68, 69, 73, 77, 80) sts. Work to 18½ (19½, 20, 20½, 21, 21½, 22)" from beg or desired length to underarm. BO rem sts in patt so flat sleeve top will fit in square armhole.

Finishing

SEW RIGHT shoulder seam. With size 7 needles and Marbella, pick up 78 (78, 78, 81, 81, 84, 84) sts around open neck edge. Work in large rib stitch for 2". Switch to size 8 needles and cont in patt for 2". Switch to size 9 needles and cont in patt for 2". BO in patt. Sew left shoulder seam along with 1" of collar. Set sleeves into armhole edges. Sew side seams, matching stripes so design will cont around sweater.

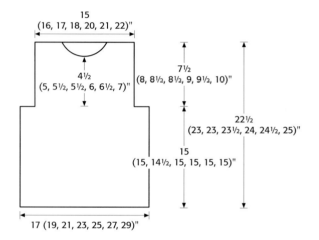

15
(16, 17, 18, 20, 21, 22)"

4½
(5, 5½, 5½, 6, 6½, 7)"

7½
(8, 8½, 8½, 9, 9½, 10)"

22½
(23, 23, 23½, 24, 24½, 25)"

15
(15, 14½, 15, 15, 15, 15)"

17 (19, 21, 23, 25, 27, 29)"

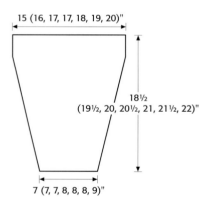

15 (16, 17, 17, 18, 19, 20)"

18½
(19½, 20, 20½, 21, 21½, 22)"

7 (7, 7, 8, 8, 8, 9)"

A CLASSICAL CONCERT

COZY, COMFORTABLE CARDIGANS

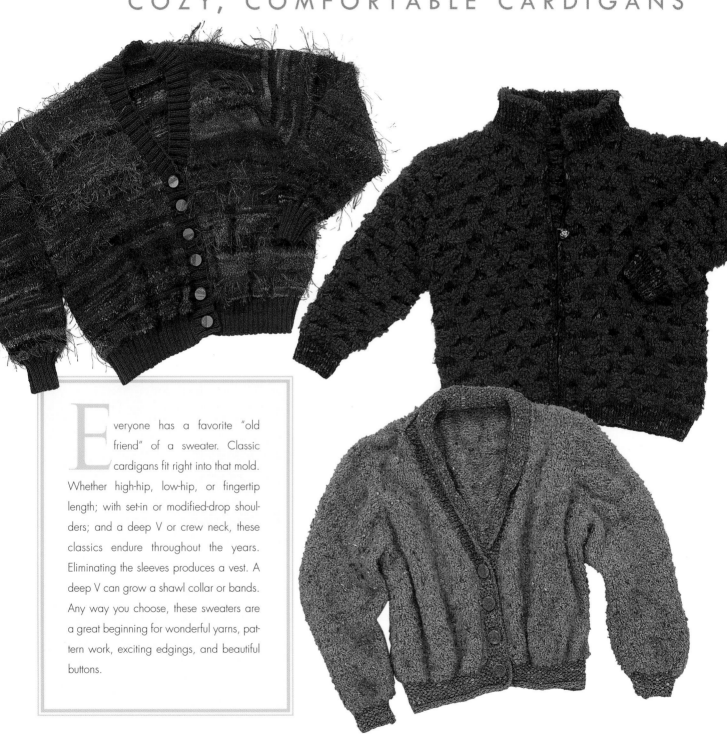

Everyone has a favorite "old friend" of a sweater. Classic cardigans fit right into that mold. Whether high-hip, low-hip, or fingertip length; with set-in or modified-drop shoulders; and a deep V or crew neck, these classics endure throughout the years. Eliminating the sleeves produces a vest. A deep V can grow a shawl collar or bands. Any way you choose, these sweaters are a great beginning for wonderful yarns, pattern work, exciting edgings, and beautiful buttons.

TUMBLING TAPESTRY

DESIGNED BY LAURA BRYANT

The rich colorations of two hand-dyed yarns give this traditional menswear vest an artistic tapestry look. The complexity of the appearance belies the simplicity of the three-stitch diagonal that moves one stitch every row. A pinstripe border with miters at the neck finishes the distinctive look. The border is fairly deep, so the armholes begin sooner, and more stitches are decreased for the neck. Adjustments are made for the "in between" gauge and the pattern repeat. Larger gauges sometimes lead you to this—feel free to "fudge" the numbers as needed!

Style: Sleeveless cardigan
Length: Low hip plus 2"
Armhole: Set-in armhole shaping
Neckline: Deep V neck

Finished Chest Measurements:
40 (44, 48, 52, 56)"

How Do I Vary from the Template?

- Gauge is between two template gauges.
- To accommodate sizing and pattern repeat, the larger gauge template was used but the numbers are taken from two sizes larger. For example, to achieve a size 40, the numbers from size 44 were used.
- Fair Isle work tends to pull stitches into a tighter stitch gauge, but the row gauge remains similar to that found in stockinette. So, the rate of decrease on the neck shaping is increased to achieve the proper number of decreases in the space allowed.
- There are two different patterns, with different repeats, so stitch counts have been adjusted for each section.
- Body length is between low hip and fingertip because it is a man's garment.

Materials

- (A)   5 (5, 6, 6, 7) skeins Prism Grain (2oz, 65yds/skein), color Embers
- (B)   4 (4, 5, 5, 6) skeins Prism Grain (2oz, 65yds/skein), color Tahoe
- Size 11 needles

- Size 13 needles (or size to obtain required gauge)
- Size H crochet hook
- 6 medium-sized buttons

Gauge

3¼ sts and 3½ rows = 1" in Fair Isle stitch on size 13 needles

Fair Isle Stitch

(Multiple of 6 plus 2)

Row 1: K1 with A, *K3 with B, K3 with A; rep from *, end K1 with B.

Row 2: *P3 with A, P3 with B; rep from *, end P2 with A.

Row 3: *K3 with A, K3 with B; rep from *, end K2 with A.

Row 4: P1 with B, *P3 with A, P3 with B; rep from *, end P1 with A.

Row 5: K2 with A, *K3 with B, K3 with A; rep from *.

Row 6: P2 with A, *P3 with B, P3 with A; rep from *.

All subsequent rows: cont in St st, moving 1 st to the right on every purl row and 1 st to the left on every knit row.

Pinstripe Border

(Even number of stitches)

Row 1: With B, *K1, sl 1 wyib; rep from *, end K2.

Row 2: With B, P2, *sl 1 wyif, P1; rep from *.

Row 3: With A, K2, *sl 1 wyib, K1; rep from *.

Row 4: With A, P1, *sl 1 wyif, P1; rep from *, end P2.

Rep rows 1–4.

Back

WITH SIZE 11 needles and A, CO 66 (72, 78, 86, 92) sts. Work pinstripe border for 2½". Switch to size 13 needles and Fair Isle stitch and work to 15 (15½, 16, 16, 16½)" from beg or desired length to underarm. Shape armholes: BO 4 (5, 6, 4, 5) sts at beg of next 2 (2, 2, 4, 4) rows, dec 1 st at each edge EOR 6 (7, 7, 7, 8) times—46 (48, 52, 56, 56) sts. Work in patt as established to 25 (25½, 26, 26, 26½)" from beg. BO rem sts.

Fronts

WITH SIZE 11 needles and A, CO 32 (36, 38, 42, 45) sts. Work pinstripe border as for back. Switch to size 13 needles and Fair Isle stitch, inc 1 (0, 1, 0, 0) st on first row. Work armhole shaping as for back at beg of RS rows, and at same time, dec 1 st at neck edge EOR 11 (11, 12, 12, 13) times. When same length as back, BO all sts. Make other front, reversing shaping, and beg Fair Isle stitch 3 sts from beg (with B instead of A) to make patt match at side seams.

Finishing

SEW SHOULDER seams. With RS facing, size 11 needles, and A, beg at side edge to pick up 68 (70, 72, 74, 76) sts around armhole edge. Attach B and work pinstripe border, beg with row 3 (since the WS is facing). Work a total of 2 rows B, 2 rows A, 2 rows B, then 1 row A. With A and WS facing, BO in purl sts. Rep for other armhole. Sew side seams. With RS facing, size 11 needles, and A, start at lower right front to pick up 48 (50, 52, 54, 56) sts to beg of neck shaping, place marker, pick up 43 (44, 45, 46, 47) sts to shoulder, 23 (24, 25, 26, 27) sts across back neck, 43 (44, 45, 46, 47) sts to beg of neck shaping, place marker, and pick up 48 (50, 52, 54, 56) sts to lower left corner. Work as for armhole edge and make neck increases on second row of B, work to marker, slip marker, work 3 sts into next st (patt maintained), work to within 1 st of next marker, work 3 sts into next st, cont in patt. Make this inc once again 4 rows later. At same time, make 6 buttonholes on left side in 5th row (counting pick-up row as row 1). Finish with 1 row A, then BO in purl sts with WS facing as for armholes. Do not cut A, and with size H crochet hook, work 1 rnd sc around entire front, neck, and bottom edges (skip every 5th st to make the edges lie flat). Work 1 rnd sc around armhole edges, working 1 st in each st. Sew buttons to right side.

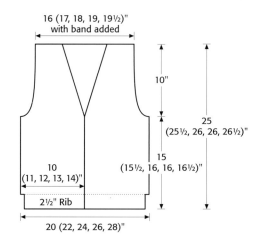

98

CLASSICAL GAS

DESIGNED BY BARRY KLEIN

lossom, the body yarn in this cardigan, is a wonderful soft-spun nylon with a bright-colored lash that comes and goes. From the moment you touch this yarn, you'll have a hard time keeping your hands off. With such a sensuous feeling, I wanted a soft jacket that could be worn today and always. For that, you need an old-fashioned shawl collar. To get the perfect collar, I decided to blend Dolcino, a woven ribbon dyed to match Blossom, and Aquarius, a bright, multicolored rayon ribbon dyed to match the accent component in Blossom. The combination is a winner.

Style: Bomber jacket
Length: Knit to low-hip length but can be pulled up when buttoned to high hip
Sleeves: Long, with set-in armhole shaping
Neckline: Deep V with shawl collar

Finished Bust Measurement:
36 (40, 44, 48, 52, 56)"

How Do I Vary from the Template?

✦ V neck shaping begins lower to accommodate shawl collar, so rates of increase are different, and more stitches are removed to provide a larger collar.

✦ Cast-on numbers for fronts include the front band stitches, which are worked with the bottom band and then placed on a holder for finishing.

✦ Sleeves have cuffs, so some of the sleeve increases are moved from the side edge to the row after the cuff, providing a blousy effect. The rate of increase along the sleeve edge is adjusted.

Materials

✦ (MC) 6 (7, 8, 9, 10, 11) skeins Trendsetter Blossom (50gr, 92yds/skein), color 100
✦ (A) 2 (2, 2, 2, 2, 3) skeins Trendsetter Dolcino (50gr, 100yds/skein), color 106
✦ (B) 2 (2, 2, 2, 2, 3) skeins Trendsetter Aquarius (50gr, 100yds/skein), color 814
✦ Size 10 needles (or size required to obtain gauge)
✦ Size H crochet hook
✦ 4 large buttons

Gauge

4 stitches and 5½ rows = 1" in stockinette stitch and MC

Knotted Rib Stitch

(Multiple of even stitches)

Row 1 (RS): With B, K1, *K1, sl 1 wyib; rep from *, end K1.

Row 2: With B, K1, *sl 1 wyif, K1; rep from *, end K1.

Row 3: With A, K1, * sl 1 wyib, K1; rep from *, end K1.

Row 4: With A, K1, *K1, sl 1 wyif; rep from *, end K1.

Back

WITH A, CO 72 (80, 88, 96, 104, 112) sts. Purl back. Work in knotted rib stitch for 2". Switch to MC and work in St st to 15 (15½, 15½, 15½, 15½, 15½)" from beg or desired length to underarm. Shape armholes: BO 4 (5, 6, 4, 5, 6) sts at beg of next 2 (2, 2, 4, 4, 4) rows. Dec 1 st at each end EOR 5 (7, 8, 8, 8, 9) times—54 (56, 60, 64, 68, 70) sts. Cont in patt until armhole is 7½ (7½, 8, 8½, 8½, 9)". BO rem sts.

Right Front

WITH SIZE 10 needles and A, CO 40 (44, 48, 52, 56, 60) sts. Purl back. Work in knotted rib stitch for 1". Make a buttonhole at ctr of first 8 sts at neck edge for front-band border. Cont in patt for 1", ending with a WS row. Work 8 sts in patt. Turn and slip 8 sts just worked to a holder at neck edge. Switch to MC and finish rem 32 (36, 40, 44, 48, 52) sts in St st. Cont in St st to 11 (11, 11½, 11½, 11½, 11½)" from beg or 4" lower than underarm shaping if you changed length on back. Mark neck edge. Cont in St st, dec 1 st at neck edge on this row and then every 5 (5, 4, 5, 4, 4) rows a total of 11 (12, 13, 13, 14, 14) times. At same time, when same length as back to underarm, BO 4 (5, 6, 4, 5, 6) sts at armhole edge 1 (1, 1, 2, 2, 2) times. Dec 1 st at armhole edge EOR 5 (7, 8, 8, 8, 9) times. Cont until armhole is same length as back and all neck shaping is complete. BO rem sts.

Left Front

WORK IN knotted rib stitch as for right front for 2" without a buttonhole and ending with a WS row. Switch to MC and work first 32 (36, 40, 44, 48, 52) sts in St st. Slip rem 8 sts to a holder at front neck edge to be worked later. Work as for right front, reversing shaping.

Sleeves

WITH SIZE 10 needles and A, CO 32 (34, 36, 36, 38, 38) sts. Purl back. Work in knotted rib stitch for 2", inc 8 (6, 6, 6, 6, 6) sts evenly across last row—40 (40, 42, 42, 44, 44) sts. Switch to MC and work in St st, inc 1 st at each end every 8 (7, 6, 6, 6, 5) rows 8 (10, 11, 11, 12, 14) times—56 (60, 64, 64, 68, 72) sts. Work to 15½ (16, 16½, 16½, 17, 17½)" from beg or desired length to underarm. Shape cap: BO 4 (5, 6, 4, 5, 6) sts at beg of next 2 rows. Dec 1 st at each end EOR until cap is 4½ (4½, 5, 5½, 5½, 6)". BO rem sts.

Finishing

SEW SHOULDER seams. Set sleeves into armhole edges. Sew side seams. With size 10 needles, pick up sts from right front holder. Cont in knotted rib stitch, making a buttonhole when 1" is worked and then every 3" up to front neck-edge marker. Reverse patt and cont, inc 1 st at each end every 7 rows 10 times. Cont until piece fits evenly along front to top of neck edge. Cont for 2¾ (3, 3¼, 3¼, 3½, 3½)" or ctr of back neck opening. BO in patt. Pick up sts from left front holder. Work in patt as for right front, but without buttonholes. BO in patt. Sew collar to front neck edge. Join at ctr back neck and reverse seam so it doesn't show. Sew buttons on left front to match buttonholes. With size H crochet hook and A, work 1 row of sc along bottom and neck edges to smooth them out and so collar lies flat.

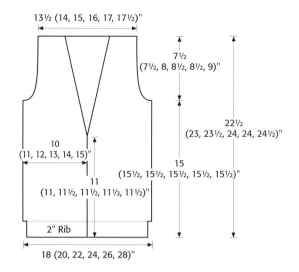

13½ (14, 15, 16, 17, 17½)"

7½ (7½, 8, 8½, 8½, 9)"

22½ (23, 23½, 24, 24, 24½)"

10 (11, 12, 13, 14, 15)"

11 (11, 11½, 11½, 11½, 11½)"

15 (15½, 15½, 15½, 15½, 15½)"

2" Rib

18 (20, 22, 24, 26, 28)"

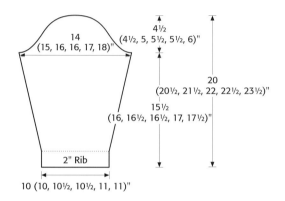

14 (15, 16, 16, 17, 18)"

4½ (4½, 5, 5½, 5½, 6)"

20 (20½, 21½, 22, 22½, 23½)"

15½ (16, 16½, 16½, 17, 17½)"

2" Rib

10 (10, 10½, 10½, 11, 11)"

WILD THING

DESIGNED BY LAURA BRYANT

Fun, flirty novelty yarns give this classic shape an updated look. Although we made ours in the low-hip length, it would be great at fingertip length and oversized. Both a crew and deep V neck are included in the pattern. I chose a very fine wool for deep ribbed cuffs and bands. To make that kind of adjustment, make a gauge swatch in rib of the finer yarn, then look at the cast-on numbers for that gauge in your size. Decrease in the first row after the rib stitch to match the template numbers.

Style:	Cardigan
Length:	Low hip
Sleeves:	Long, with set-in armhole shaping
Neckline:	Deep V or crew neck

Finished Bust Measurement:
36 (40, 44, 48, 52)"

How Do I Vary from the Template?

✦ The ribbed borders are a much finer gauge than the body, so cast on numbers are adjusted. The stitches are decreased in the first row of the body.

✦ The sleeve cuff is quite deep, so fewer stitches are decreased when the cuff is finished, allowing for a fuller, slightly blousy sleeve. The rate of increase along the edge is adjusted so that the correct number of stitches is achieved when the cap is reached.

✦ Shoulders are shaped for better fit.

Materials

✦ 3 (3½, 4, 4½, 5) skeins Prism Wild Stuff (6–8 oz, 300yds/skein), color Autumn for V neck or color Nevada for crew neck

✦ 2 (2, 2, 3) skeins Lane Borgosesia Merino Sei, (50gr, 137yds/skein), color 25278

✦ Size 2 needles

✦ Size 8 needles (or size required to obtain gauge)

✦ 6 medium buttons

Gauge

4½ stitches and 6½ rows = 1" in stockinette stitch with Wild Stuff on size 8 needles

Rib Stitch

(Multiple of 4 plus 2; to allow for edge sts)

Row 1: *K2, P2; rep from *, end K2.
Row 2: P2, *K2, P2; rep from *.
Rep rows 1 and 2.

Back

WITH MERINO Sei and size 2 needles, CO 98 (110, 134, 146, 158) sts. Work in rib stitch for 3". Switch to size 8 needles and Wild Stuff. Work in St st, dec 16 (20, 34, 38, 40) sts evenly across first row—82 (90, 100, 108, 118) sts. Work in St st to 15 (15½, 15½, 15½, 15½)" from beg or desired length to underarm. Shape armholes: BO 5 (5, 6, 5, 5) sts at beg of next 2 (2, 2, 4, 4) rows, dec 1 st at each edge EOR 6 (9, 10, 8, 10) times—60 (62, 68, 72, 78) sts. Work to 22½ (23, 23½, 24, 24)" from beg. BO 9 (9, 10, 7, 7) sts at beg of next 4 rows, BO 0 (0, 0, 7, 9) sts at beg of next 2 rows. BO rem sts.

Fronts

WITH MERINO Sei and size 2 needles, CO 46 (54, 66, 70, 74) sts. Work in rib stitch as for back to 3". Switch to size 8 needles and Wild Stuff. Work in St st, dec 5 (9, 16, 16, 15) sts evenly across first row until 41 (45, 50, 54, 59) sts rem.

V neck: Work as for back to 14½". Shape neck: Dec 1 st at neck edge only every 4 rows 12 (13, 14, 15, 16) times. At same time, when same length as back to underarm, shape armhole as for back at side edge only. When same length as back, shape shoulders as for back.

Crew neck: When armhole is 5 (5, 5½, 6, 6)", shape neck: At neck edge only, BO 12 (12, 14, 14, 14,) sts once, BO 3 sts once, BO 2 (2, 2, 3, 3) sts once, dec 1 (2, 2, 2, 3) sts once. When front is same length as back, shape shoulders as for back.

Make other front, reversing shaping.

Sleeves

WITH SIZE 2 needles and Merino Sei, CO 42 (42, 46, 46, 50) sts. Work in rib stitch for 3". Switch to size 8 needles and Wild Stuff. Work in St st, dec 2 (2, 2, 0, 2) sts evenly across first row—40 (40, 44, 46, 48) sts. (There are only a few decreases here, to allow the sleeve to blouse slightly over the cuff.) Working in St st, inc 1 st at each edge every 6 rows 12 (14, 14, 14, 15) times—64 (68, 72, 74, 78) sts. Work to 15½ (16, 16½, 16½, 17)" or desired length to underarm. Shape cap: BO 5 (5, 6, 5, 5) sts at beg of next 2 rows. Dec 1 st at each edge EOR to a cap depth of 4½ (4½, 5, 5½, 5½)". BO rem sts.

Finishing

SEW SHOULDER seams. Sew side and sleeve seams. Set sleeves into armhole edges.

V neck

Front bands: With size 2 needles and Merino Sei, beg at right front lower corner and pick up 75 (77, 77, 79, 79) sts to 1 st before beg of V shaping, place marker, pick up 2 sts, place marker, pick up 55 (57, 58, 59, 59) sts to shoulder seam, 42 (42, 44, 46) 46 sts along back neck, 55 (57, 58, 59, 59) sts to 1 st before V shaping, place marker, pick up 2 sts, place marker, pick up 75 (77, 77, 79, 79) sts to bottom edge. Work in P2, K2 rib (beg with purl st since you are beg on WS) for 7 rows, making miter increases every 4 rows: work to within 1 st of marker, inc 1 st in that st, slip marker, K2, slip

NOTE: The rib can be flattened slightly with light steam to remove some of the elasticity and to prevent the band from pulling up.

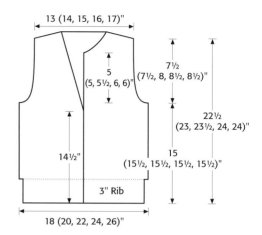

13 (14, 15, 16, 17)"

5 (5, 5½, 6, 6)"

7½ (7½, 8, 8½, 8½)"

22½ (23, 23½, 24, 24)"

14½"

15 (15½, 15½, 15½, 15½)"

3" Rib

18 (20, 22, 24, 26)"

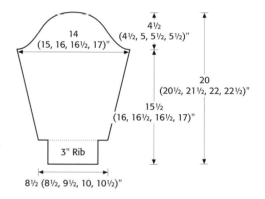

14 (15, 16, 16½, 17)"

4½ (4½, 5, 5½, 5½)"

20 (20½, 21½, 22, 22½)"

15½ (16, 16½, 16½, 17)"

3" Rib

8½ (8½, 9½, 10, 10½)"

marker, inc 1 st in next st. Work these sts into patt as pos-sible, always keeping the 2 sts between the markers in St st. At same time, in 8th row, make 6 buttonholes in right band. Finish 8 more rows, cont to inc every 4 rows on each side of each mark-er. BO in rib. Sew buttons to left band.

Crew neck

Front bands: With size 2 needles and Merino Sei, pick up 118 (120, 122, 124, 126) sts along left front. Work in P2, K2 rib (beg with purl st since you are beg on WS) for 1½". BO smoothly in rib. Mark for 5 buttons. Make right front band as for left front band, making buttonholes halfway through band, approximately ¾" from body, and corresponding to marks on left front band.

Collar band: With size 2 needles and Merino Sei, pick up 82 (86, 90, 94, 94) sts around neck edge. Work K2, P2 rib for 1½", working 1 buttonhole at right front corner. BO sts in rib, making sure collar band lies flat. Sew buttons to left side.

DIAMONDS ARE FOREVER

DESIGNED BY BARRY KLEIN

I love playing with texture differences and color subtleties. The classic bomber jacket shows off this interplay beautifully. An easy slip-stitch pattern creates diamonds with yarns that are different in color and texture. The zipper up the front creates a nice smooth line, allowing the jacket to be worn at low hip or pulled up to high hip, which blouses the fabric a bit. As always, follow our gauge charts and make the easy changes to get the look you want.

Style: Bomber jacket
Length: Low hip
Sleeve: Long, with modified-drop armhole shaping
Neckline: Crew neck

Finished Bust Measurement:
36 (40, 45, 49, 54)"

How Do I Vary from the Template?

+ Stitches and sizing are adjusted for pattern repeat.
+ Cuff is deep, so some increases are made in the row after border for a bloused effect. Also, the row gauge is different, so adjustments are made to the number and rate of increases along sleeve edge.

Materials

+ (A) 5 (5, 6, 6, 7) skeins Trendsetter Dolce (50g, 100yds/skein), color 1
+ (B) 6 (7, 8, 9, 10) skeins Trendsetter Zucca (50g, 72yds/skein), color 5060
+ Size 10 needles
+ Size 10½ needles (or size to obtain required gauge)
+ Size H crochet hook
+ Zipper (length of front up to shaping)

Gauge

3½ stitches and 5 rows = 1" in diamond slip stitch on size 10½ needles

Rib Stitch

Row 1: *K1, P1; rep from *.
Row 2: Work stitches as they face you.
Rep rows 1 and 2.

Diamond Slip Stitch

(Multiple of 8 plus 6)

Row 1 (RS): With B, knit.
Row 2: With B, K6, *sl 2 wyif, K6; rep from *.
Row 3: With B, K6, *sl 2 wyib, K6; rep from *.
Row 4: Rep row 2.
Row 5: With A, K6, *sl 2 wyib, K6; rep from *.
Row 6: With A, P6, *sl 2 wyif, P6; rep from *.
Row 7: Rep row 5.
Row 8: Rep row 6.
Row 9: With B, knit.
Row 10: With B, K2, *sl 2 wyif, K6; rep from *, end sl 2 wyif, K2.
Row 11: With B, K2, *sl 2 wyib, K6; rep from *, end sl 2 wyib, K2.
Row 12: With B, rep row 10.

Row 13: With A, K2, *sl 2 wyib, K6; rep from *, end sl 2 wyib, K2.

Row 14: With A, P2, *sl 2 wyif, P6; rep from *, end sl 2 wyif, P2.

Rep rows 1–14.

Back

WITH SIZE 10 needles and A, CO 62 (68, 74, 80, 86) sts. Work in rib stitch for 2", inc 0 (2, 4, 6, 8) sts evenly across last row—62 (70, 78, 86, 94) sts. Switch to size 10½ needles and work in diamond slip stitch to 14½ (15, 15, 15, 15)" from beg or desired length to underarm. Shape armholes: BO 6 (7, 9, 9, 11) sts at beg of next 2 rows—50 (56, 60, 68, 72) sts. Cont in patt, as possible, until armhole is 8 (8, 8½, 9, 9½)". BO rem sts in patt.

Fronts

WORK BOTH fronts at same time, cont in patt from one front to next; wherever you are in patt, just cont on second front.

With size 10 needles and A, CO 31 (34, 37, 40, 43) sts for each front. Work in rib stitch for 2", inc 0 (1, 2, 3, 4) sts evenly across last row—31 (35, 39, 43, 47) sts for each front. Switch to size 10½ needles and work in diamond slip stitch until fronts are same length to underarm as back. BO 6 (7, 9, 9, 11) sts at each armhole edge once. Cont in patt as possible until armhole is 5 (5, 5½, 6, 6½)". Shape neck: At each neck edge, BO 5 (5, 5, 5, 6) sts once, BO 2 (3, 3, 3, 3) sts once, BO 2 sts once, dec 1 st once. Cont until armhole is same length as back. BO rem sts.

Sleeves

WITH SIZE 10 needles and A, CO 24 (24, 26, 28, 30) sts. Work in rib stitch for 2", inc 6 (6, 12, 10, 8) sts evenly across last row—30 (30, 38, 38, 38) sts. Switch to size 10½ needles and work in diamond

slip stitch, inc 1 st at each end every 5 (5, 6, 5, 5) rows 10 (11, 9, 11, 11) times, working new sts into patt, as possible—50 (52, 56, 60, 60) sts. Work in patt, as possible, to 15½ (16, 16½, 17, 17)" from beg or desired length to underarm. Shape cap: BO 2 sts at beg of next 16 rows. BO rem sts.

Finishing

SEW SHOULDER seams. With size 10 needles and A, pick up 70 (72, 72, 74, 74) sts around neck edge. Work in rib stitch for 2½". Switch to B and knit 1 row. Change back to A and work in rib stitch for 2½". BO sts in patt. Fold collar to inside and tack in place at collar pick-up. Set sleeves into armhole edges. Sew side seams. With size H crochet hook and A, work 2 rows of sc along front edge. Tack zipper to inside of each front edge just inside crocheted edge. Sew in place up to edge of neck shaping.

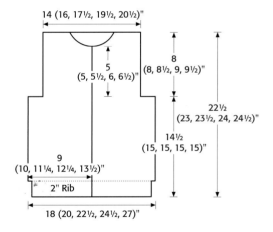

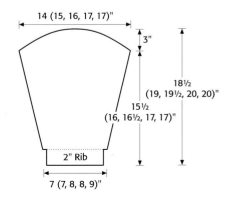

TAILOR MADE

Elegant tailored jackets say it all. From office to evening, these often buttonless jackets are usually straight in shape and high or low hip in length. Necklines of V or crew shaping allow for interesting band details and collar possibilities. Since the center fronts meet rather than overlap, this is a good style choice for adding a zipper.

BRIGHT LIGHTS, BIG CITY

DESIGNED BY BARRY KLEIN

This style of jacket calls out for texture, glitter, and excitement. By using three different yarns, each with a different texture and color, you can show all of these effects. In this jacket, I used each yarn for one row only, thus each yarn is in the right place and ready to use again. To avoid any kind of narrow striping, I used seed stitch, which adds another texture and makes the knitting resemble fabric, allowing colors and textures to move in and out. The sleeves are knit a bit longer than normal and then folded back, creating a cuff that finishes the look.

Style: Cardigan
Length: High hip
Sleeves: Long, with set-in armhole
            shaping
Neckline: Jewel neck

Finished Bust Measurement:
36 (40, 44, 48, 52, 56)"

How Do I Vary from the Template?
+   Stitches are adjusted for pattern
    repeat.
+   Sleeve has a folded back cuff,
    which requires more stitches and longer
    length, and alters the rate of increase
    along the edge.

Materials

+   (A)   5 (5, 6, 6, 7, 7) skeins Trendsetter
    Sunshine (50g, 95yds/skein), color 74
+   (B)   4 (4, 5, 5, 6, 6) skeins Trendsetter
    Binario (25g, 82yds/skein), color 101
+   (C)   4 (4, 4, 5, 5, 5) skeins Trendsetter
    Aura (50g, 150yds/skein), color 3170
+   Size 7 needles
+   Size F crochet hook

Gauge

5½ stitches and 7½ rows = 1" in seed stitch

Seed Stitch

(Odd number of stitches)

Row 1: *K1, P1; rep from *, end K1.
Row 2: *K1, P1; rep from *, end K1.
Rep rows 1 and 2.

NOTE: Pattern is worked with 1 row of each yarn. Cast on with A, drop A and attach B, work across with B, drop B, attach C, work across with C, and A is waiting to be worked again.

Back

WITH A, CO 99 (109, 119, 131, 141, 153) sts. Work in seed stitch, using each yarn for 1 row only and bringing yarns up as you work. Work to 13 (13½, 13½, 13½, 13½, 13½)" from beg or desired length to underarm. Shape armholes: BO 5 (6, 6, 4, 5, 6) sts at beg of next 2 (2, 2, 4, 4, 4) rows. Dec 1 st at each end EOR 7 (10, 13, 14, 14, 17) times— 75 (77, 81, 87, 93, 95) sts. Cont until armhole is 7½ (7½, 8, 8½, 8½, 9)". BO rem sts in patt.

Fronts

WITH A, CO 51 (55, 59, 65, 71, 77) sts. Work in seed stitch as for back until same length to underarm. Shape armhole: BO 5 (6, 6, 4, 5, 6) sts at armhole edge 1 (1, 1, 2, 2, 2) times. Dec 1 st at armhole edge EOR 7 (10, 13, 14, 14, 17) times—39 (39, 40, 43, 47, 48) sts. At same time, when armhole is 4 (4, 4½, 5, 5, 5½)", shape neck: At neck edge only, BO 7 (8, 10, 10, 10, 10) sts once. BO 3 sts twice. Dec 1 st at neck edge EOR 2 (2, 2, 2, 3, 3) times. Cont until front is same length as back to shoulder. BO rem sts in patt. Make second front, reversing shaping.

Sleeves

WITH A, CO 43 (47, 49, 51, 53, 53) sts. Work in seed st, inc 1 st at each end every 7 (8, 8, 7, 7, 7) rows 17 (16, 17, 18, 19, 20) times and working new sts into patt—77 (79, 83, 87, 91, 93) sts. Work to 18 (18½, 18½, 19, 19½, 20)" from beg or desired length to underarm. Shape cap: BO 5 (6, 6, 4, 5, 6) sts at beg of next 2 rows. Dec 1 st at each end EOR until cap is 4½ (4½, 5, 5½, 5½, 6)". BO rem sts in patt.

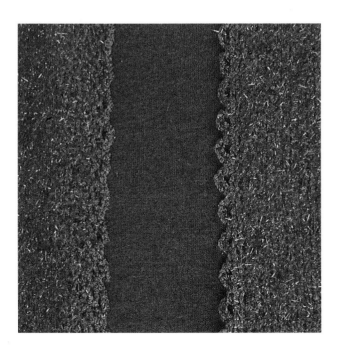

Finishing

SEW SHOULDER seams. Set sleeves into armhole edge. With size F crochet hook and Sunshine, work the following 3-row crochet along bottom, front, and neck edges. Rep for edge of sleeve cuff only.

Rows 1 and 2: Sc.
Row 3: *Ch 3 and sc into next st; rep from * to create scalloped edge. Fasten off.

Sew side seams. Try on jacket and fold up sleeve cuff; tack in place with a pin. Sew sleeve seam, reversing the seam at cuff fold line. Permanently tack sleeve cuff in place.

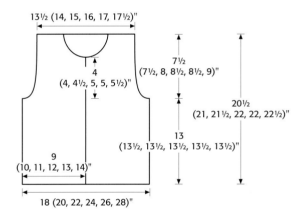

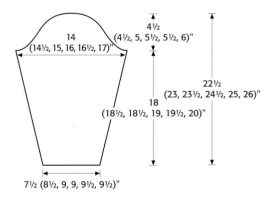

113

BAROQUE BALLAD

DESIGNED BY LAURA BRYANT

This elegantly tailored jacket combines several of my favorite elements: the half linen stitch and three compatible but different yarns. The rich "woven" texture keeps the fabric flat, allowing the finish to be a simple I-cord and garter-stitch edge. The flecks of metallic and dyed gold rayon shine like gold leaf, while the deep, rich colors are reminiscent of jewels. The edge flows beautifully over the shallow V neck and continues down the front and completely around the bottom. The shoulders are slightly shaped for a better fit. Make a size larger than you think you want, to make sure the fronts hang correctly without gapping.

Style: Jacket

Length: Low hip

Sleeves: Long, with set-in armhole shaping

Neckline: Shallow V neck

Finished Bust Measurement:

36 (40, 44, 48, 52)"

How Do I Vary from the Template?

✦ Stitches are adjusted for pattern repeat.

✦ Shoulders are shaped.

✦ Sleeves are knit ½" shorter to allow for added border.

Materials

✦ (A) 6 (6, 7, 8, 8) skeins Prism Lunette (1 oz/63yds), color Embers

✦ (B) 6 (6, 7, 8, 8) skeins Prism Luna (1 oz/58yds), color Yosemite

✦ (C) 6 (6, 7, 8, 8) skeins Prism Diana (1 oz/55yds), color Cabernet

✦ Size 13 straight needles (or size required to obtain gauge)

✦ Size 10½ circular needle (36")

Gauge

3½ stitches and 7½ rows = 1" in half linen stitch on size 13 needles

Half Linen Stitch

(Odd number of stitches)

Row 1: *K1, sl 1 wyif; rep from *, end K1.
Rows 2 and 4: Purl.
Row 3: K2, *sl 1 wyif, K1; rep from *, end K1.
Rep rows 1–4.

NOTE: Work 1 row of each yarn as follows: CO with A, drop A and attach B, work across with B, drop B, attach C, work across with C, and A is waiting at the other end.

Back

WITH SIZE 13 needles and A, CO 64 (70, 78, 84, 92) sts. Work in half linen stitch with color rep to 15 (15½, 15½, 15½, 15½)" or desired length to underarm. Shape armholes: BO 4 (5, 5, 5, 3) sts at beg of next 2 (2, 2, 2, 4) rows. Dec 1 st at each edge EOR 4 (5, 8, 9, 10) times—48 (50, 52, 56, 60) sts. Work to 22½ (23, 23½, 24, 24)" from beg. Shape shoulders: BO 4 (5, 5, 5, 6) sts at beg of next 4 rows. BO 6 (5, 6, 7, 6) sts at beg of next 2 rows. BO rem sts.

Fronts

WITH SIZE 13 needles and A, CO 32 (36, 40, 42, 46) sts. Work in half linen stitch as for back to armhole. Shape armhole at side edge only. Work to 17 (17½, 18, 18½, 18½)" from beg. Shape neck: dec 1 st at ctr edge EOR 10 (11, 11, 11, 12) times. When same length as back to shoulder, shape shoulders as for back. Work second front, reversing shaping.

Sleeves

WITH SIZE 13 needles and A, CO 24 (24, 26, 28, 30) sts. Work in half linen stitch as for body, inc 1 st at each edge every 6 (6, 6, 6, 5) rows 13 (14, 14, 14, 15) times—50 (52, 54, 56, 60) sts. Work to 15 (15½, 16, 16, 16½)" from beg or desired length to underarm less ½". Shape cap: BO 4 (5, 5, 5, 3) sts at beg of next 2 rows. Dec 1 st at each edge EOR to cap depth of 4½ (4½, 5, 5½, 5½)". BO rem sts.

Sleeve edging: With size 10½" circular needle and B, pick up 24 (26, 28, 30, 30) sts along bottom edge. Knit 1 row, then add A and knit 2 rows. Cut A, pick up B, and knit 2 more rows. Beg applied I-cord: CO 3 sts with A, then *knit 2 sts, then SSK with the last A st and the first B st at sleeve bottom. Slide the 3 sts back to left needle, pull yarn tightly around back, and rep from *. When 1 B st remains, BO A sts as you work last row. Rep for other sleeve.

Finishing

BODY EDGE is worked in one continuous row, which means there will be a lot of stitches on the needle at once, and the corners will seem a bit awkward. Trust us, it works, and it makes a great finish. Sew side and shoulder seams. With size 10½

circular needle and B, beg at left side seam, pick up 62 (68, 75, 80, 90) sts along back bottom edge, 30 (34, 38, 40, 44) sts along front bottom edge, place marker, pick up 64 (64, 66, 68, 68) sts to beg of neck shaping, place marker, pick up 30 sts to shoulder seam, 20 (22, 22, 24, 24) sts along back neck, 30 sts to neck shaping, place marker, pick up 64 (64, 66, 68, 68) sts to bottom, place marker, and pick up 30 (34, 38, 40, 44) sts to side seam. Turn and knit 1 row. Drop B and attach C and knit 2 rows: In the first row, inc 1 st on either side of markers at bottom edges, inc 1 st only at each neck edge (1 after first marker and 1 before 2nd marker), and dec 1 st at each shoulder seam. Turn and knit 1 row. Fasten off C. Knit 2 rows B, working increases as for C. Fasten off B. Cast on 3 sts with A and work applied I-cord as for sleeve, working bottom corners as follows: When you reach marker, K3 (omitting the SSK), sl 3 sts back to left needle, K2, SSK, rep K3 row with no SSK, work normally to neck edge, remove marker, and work one K3 row with no SSK, then return to K2, SSK.

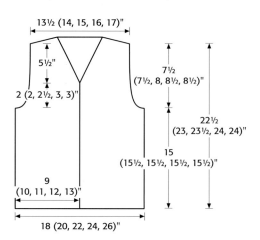

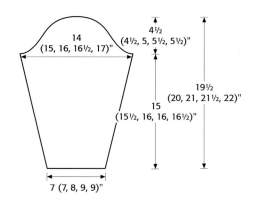

LASHING OUT

DESIGNED BY BARRY KLEIN

Y ou just want to run your fingers through the lashes—the feeling is so wonderful. The paper-lash component is light and free-flowing, and by blending a multicolored eyelash, the yarn gets a bit thicker and more colors come out. I decided to taper this cropped jacket to keep the fullness of the lashes away from the hips. Note that the lashes really changed the standard stitch-row gauge ratio, bringing the body and sleeve increases closer together.

Style: Jacket

Length: Cropped

Taper: Narrower waist to wider bust

Sleeves: Long, with set-in armhole shaping

Neckline: Boat neck that folds back

Finished Bust Measurement:
34 (38, 42, 46, 50)"

How Do I Vary from the Template?

✦ Row gauge is different, so rate of taper on body and increases on sleeves are adjusted.

Materials

✦ 10 (11, 13, 15, 17) skeins Trendsetter Papi (25g, 70yds/skein), color 24

✦ 10 (11, 12, 14, 15) skeins Trendsetter Shadow (20g, 77yds/skein), color 470

NOTE: Main color (MC) is 1 strand of Papi and 1 strand of Shadow held together.

✦ 1 (1, 1, 1, 1) skein Trendsetter Dolcino (50g, 100yds/skein), color 101

✦ Size 10 needles (or size required to obtain gauge)

✦ Size H crochet hook

Gauge

4½ stitches and 6 rows = 1" in reverse stockinette stitch with MC

Back

With Dolcino, CO 68 (76, 84, 94, 102) sts loosely. Switch to MC and work in rev St st, inc 1 st at each end every 15 (13, 13, 13, 13) rows 4 (5, 5, 5, 5) times—76 (86, 94, 104, 112) sts. Work to 11½" from beg or desired length to underarm. Shape armholes: BO 4 (5, 5, 6, 5) sts at beg of next 2 (2, 2, 2, 4) rows. Dec 1 st at each end EOR 4 (7, 10, 11, 9) times—60 (62, 64, 70, 74) sts. Cont until armhole is 7 (7½, 8, 8, 8½)". BO rem sts.

Fronts

With Dolcino, CO 34 (38, 42, 47, 51) sts loosely. Switch to MC and work in rev St st, inc 1 st at armhole edge every 15 (13, 13, 13, 13) rows 4 (5, 5, 5, 5) times—38 (43, 47, 52, 56) sts. Work until body is same length as back to underarm. BO 4 (5, 5, 6, 5) sts at armhole edge 1 (1, 1, 1, 2) times. Dec 1 st at armhole edge EOR 4 (7, 10, 11, 9) times. When armhole is same as for back, BO 18 (19, 20, 20, 21) sts at neck edge. BO rem sts. Make other front, reversing shaping.

Sleeves

WITH DOLCINO, CO 28 (32, 32, 36, 40) sts. Switch to MC and work in rev St st, inc 1 st at each end every 4 (5, 5, 5, 5) rows 17 (17, 18, 18, 18) times—62 (66, 68, 72, 76) sts. Work to 15½ (16, 16, 16½, 17)" from beg or desired length to underarm. Shape cap: BO 4 (5, 5, 6, 5) sts at beg of next 2 rows. Dec 1 st at each end EOR until cap is 4 (4½, 5, 5, 5½)". BO rem sts.

Finishing

SEW SHOULDER seams, working from armhole edge toward neck and stopping at neck bind-off. Set sleeves into armhole edge. Sew underarm and side seams. With size H crochet hook and Dolcino, join yarn at bottom front edge and work 1 row of sc around front and neck edges. Work back with 1 row of slip stitch, working through front half of stitch only, and continue around cast-on edge of front and back.

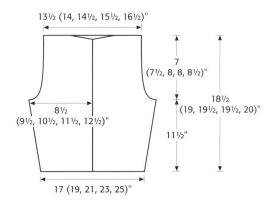

13½ (14, 14½, 15½, 16½)"

7 (7½, 8, 8, 8½)"

18½ (19, 19½, 19½, 20)"

8½ (9½, 10½, 11½, 12½)"

11½"

17 (19, 21, 23, 25)"

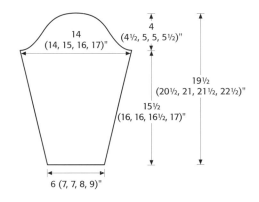

4 (4½, 5, 5, 5½)"

14 (14, 15, 16, 17)"

19½ (20½, 21, 21½, 22½)"

15½ (16, 16, 16½, 17)"

6 (7, 7, 8, 9)"

ZIPPERED ZEBRA

DESIGNED BY LAURA BRYANT

A love of velvety chenille and a desire to tame its sometimes unruly characteristics led to this dressy jacket. The tailored style has reverse taper from the waist to the underarm, slim set-in sleeves, and a slightly shorter than high-hip length to give a very close fit. Crew-neck shaping provides the base for a mitered collar. Linen stitch controls the chenille, stopping any potential worming and providing a firm, flat fabric. A simple single crochet/reverse single crochet edge is the perfect finish, with a ready-made "ditch" into which you can stitch the rhinestone zipper. With a long, slim skirt or tailored pants, this jacket defines elegance and fun!

Style: Jacket
Length: High hip less ½"
Taper: Narrower waist to wider bust
Sleeves: Long, with set-in armhole shaping
Neckline: Crew neck with attached collar

Finished Bust Measurement:
36 (40, 44, 48, 52)"

How Do I Vary from the Template?
+ Neck shaping is smaller for a closer fitting collar.
+ Shoulder shaping is added since the fit is so close.
+ Cuff is a larger gauge, so adjustments are made in the cast on, and in increases made after the cuff.
+ Length is between cropped and high-hip.

Materials

+ 13 (14, 17, 19, 21) balls Muench Touch Me, (50gr, 61yds/skein), color black
+ 2 (2, 2, 2, 2) skeins Prism Fern (2oz, 58yds/skein), color Zebra
+ 16 (16, 18, 18, 18)" Rhinestone zipper (available from Great Yarns)
+ Size 8 needles
+ Size 10 needles (or size required to obtain gauge)
+ Size G crochet hook

Gauge

5 stitches and 7½ rows = 1" in linen stitch on size 10 needles

Linen Stitch

(Even number of stitches)

Row 1: *K1, sl 1 wyif; rep from *, end K2.
Row 2: *P1, sl 1 wyib; rep from *, end K2.

NOTE: Before measuring gauge or length of knitting, grasp the knitting firmly at top and bottom and pull hard to "set" linen stitch correctly. Lightly pull from side to side, then measure.

Back

WITH SIZE 8 needles and Touch Me, CO 80 (90, 100, 108, 118) sts. Switch to size 10 needles and work in linen stitch, inc 1 st at each edge every 14 (14, 16, 14, 14) rows a total of 5 (5, 5, 6, 6) times—90 (100, 110, 120, 130) sts. Work to 12½

(13, 13, 13, 13)" from beg or desired length to underarm. Shape armholes: BO 5 (5, 6, 4, 5) sts at beg of next 2 (2, 2, 4, 4) rows. Dec 1 st at each edge EOR 6 (10, 12, 12, 13) times—68 (70, 76, 82, 84) sts. Work to 20 (20½, 21, 21½, 21½)" from beg. Shape shoulders: BO 4 sts in patt at beg of next 10 (10, 8, 12, 10) rows, then BO 0 (0, 6, 0, 5) sts in patt at beg of next 0 (0, 2, 0, 2) rows.

Fronts

WITH SIZE 8 needles and Touch Me, CO 40 (46, 50, 56, 64) sts. Switch to size 10 needles and work in linen stitch, inc 1 st at beg of RS row every 2" a total of 5 (5, 5, 6, 6) times—45 (51, 55, 62, 70) sts. When same length as back to underarm, shape armhole at beg of RS rows. When piece is 16 (16, 18, 18, 18)" from beg, shape neck: At beg of next WS row, BO 7 (7, 8, 8, 8) sts. At neck edge, BO 3 sts once, 2 sts once, dec 1 st EOR 2 (2, 2, 2, 3) times. When piece is same length as back to shoulder, shape shoulders as for back at beg of RS rows only. Make other front, reversing shaping.

Sleeves

WITH SIZE 8 needles and Fern, CO 26 (28, 30, 32, 34) sts. Working garter st for 2", switch to Touch Me, and knit 1 row, inc 14 (16, 18, 16, 16) sts evenly across row—40 (44, 48, 48, 50) sts. Switch to size 10 needles and work in linen stitch, inc 1 st at each edge every 6 rows 15 (15, 17, 17, 18) times—70 (74, 82, 84, 86) sts. Work to 15½ (16, 16½, 16½, 17)" from beg or desired length to underarm. Shape cap: BO 5 (5, 6, 4, 5) sts at beg of next 2 rows. Dec 1 st at each edge EOR to cap depth of 4½ (4½, 5, 5½, 5½)". BO rem sts.

Collar

WITH SIZE 8 needles and Fern, CO 82 (84, 84, 86, 86) sts. Knit 2 rows.

Next row: K9, sl 1, K2tog, psso, K58 (60, 60, 62, 62), K3tog, K9.

Next row and all alternate rows: Knit.

Next row: K8, sl 1, K2tog, psso, K56 (58, 58, 60, 60), K3tog, K8.

Next dec row: K7, sl 1, K2tog, psso, work to within 10 sts, K3tog, K7. Cont in this manner, working 1 less st at beg, 2 less sts in middle, and 1 less st at end. Work until all of original 9 sts at each end have been used. BO rem sts.

Finishing

SEW SHOULDER seams firmly. Sew side and sleeve seams. Set sleeves into armhole edges. With size G crochet hook, work 1 rnd sc and 1 rnd rev sc around entire bottom, front, and neck edges. Work 2 rows sc along cast-on edge (including turned edge) of collar. Set zipper into front edge, basting by hand and then stitching by machine in the ditch between the sc and rev sc. Sew collar to neck edge, placing collar inside of crocheted edge and topstitching by hand through sc row of both collar and neck.

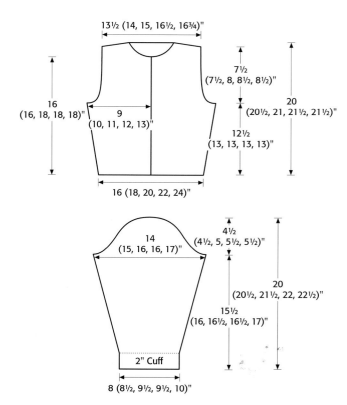

THE FINAL COAT

THE BEST LAYER OF ALL

Knitted coats remain a favorite of couture designers and knitters alike. What could be better than a warm cozy coat on a cold day? Fingertip to long, these coats have tapered shaping from hem to armhole, which allows for proper fit and drape. Lots of collar and neckline options will work, and the sleeves can even be eliminated for a dressy evening vest!

WILD WAVES

DESIGNED BY BARRY KLEIN

This coat is based on the colors of my favorite mohair tweed. While knitting a stockinette-stitch swatch, I noticed the colors looked like waves. By blending solid ribbons in a chevron pattern, the design got even wavier. I just love working this garter chevron pattern and so I varied the striping by working different widths in the body, sleeves, and collar. I wanted a coat somewhere between fingertip and long and not quite as full as our standard taper. Because this pattern has a big multiple, the solution was to change needle sizes to create extra ease and provide taper. Finally, the sleeve is a bit longer so you can turn it up and let the chevron edge show as a cuff border.

Style: Coat

Length: Between fingertip and long

Taper: Taper created by needle-size changes

Sleeves: Long, with square armhole shaping and straight bind-off

Neckline: Crew neck

Finished Bust Measurement:

40 (44, 48, 53, 56)"

How Do I Vary from the Template?

✦ Swing is built in by changing needle size, and thus gauge.

✦ Stitches are adjusted for very large pattern repeat.

✦ Sleeve has a folded back cuff, which requires more stitches and longer length, and alters the rate of increase along the edge.

Materials

✦ (MC) 5 (6, 7, 7, 8) skeins Trendsetter Dune (50g, 90yds/skein), color 92

✦ (A) 5 (6, 7, 7, 8) skeins Trendsetter Dolcino (50g, 100yds/skein), color 30

✦ (B) 4 (5, 5, 6, 7) skeins Trendsetter Dolcino, (50g, 100yds/skein), color 8

✦ (C) 4 (5, 5, 6, 7) skeins Trendsetter Dolcino, (50g, 100yds/skein), color 106

✦ Size 9 needles

✦ Size 10 needles (or size required to obtain gauge)

✦ Size 10½ needles

✦ Size 11 needles

✦ Size H crochet hook

✦ 3 large buttons

Gauge

5 stitches and 6½ rows = 1" in garter chevron pattern on size 10 needles

Garter Chevron Pattern

(Multiple of 16 [18, 20, 16, 18] plus 3)

Row 1 (RS): K1, *K1, YO, K6 (7, 8, 6, 7), sl 1 wyib, K2tog, psso, K6 (7, 8, 6, 7), YO; rep from *, end K2.

Row 2: K2, *P1, K13 (15, 17, 13, 15), P2; rep from *, end K1.

Rep rows 1 and 2.

Large Stripe Sequence

18 rows A
2 rows C
18 rows B
2 rows MC
18 rows C
2 rows A
18 rows MC
2 rows B

Small Stripe Sequence

8 rows A
2 rows C
8 rows B
2 rows MC
8 rows C
2 rows A
8 rows MC
2 rows B

Back

WITH SIZE 11 needles and MC, CO 99 (111, 123, 131, 147) sts. Knit back. Beg large stripe sequence in garter chevron patt. Cont in stripe sequence and patt until 8" from beg. Switch to size 10½ needles for 8". Switch to size 10 needles for 8". Switch to size 9 needles for balance of back. At same time, when 26 (27, 28, 29, 30)" from beg or desired length to underarm, shape armholes: BO 10 (12, 13, 15, 17) sts at beg of next 2 rows—79 (87, 97, 101, 113) sts. Cont until armhole is 8 (8, 8½, 9, 9)". BO rem sts firmly.

Fronts

WITH SIZE 11 needles and MC, CO 51 (57, 63, 67, 75) sts. Knit back. Work as follows: 3 sts garter st at neck edge, 48 (54, 60, 64, 72) sts in garter chevron patt and stripe sequence while changing needles as for back. When 26 (27, 28, 29, 30)" from beg or same length as back to underarm, BO 8 (12, 14, 15, 21) sts at armhole edge once—43 (45, 49, 52, 54) sts. Cont until armhole is 5 (5½, 6, 6, 6½)". BO 7 (8, 8, 8, 8) sts at neck edge once. BO 3 sts at neck edge twice. Dec 1 st at neck edge EOR 2 (2, 2, 3, 3) times—28 (29, 33, 35, 37) sts. Cont until armhole is 8 (8, 8½, 9, 9)". BO rem sts firmly. Make second front, working Chevron st on first 48 (54, 60, 64, 72) sts and garter st on last 3 sts for front edge, and reversing shaping.

Sleeves

WITH SIZE 10 needles and MC, CO 51 sts. Knit back. Beg small stripe sequence in garter chevron patt, using smallest size for all sizes. Cont in stripe sequence and patt, inc 1 st at each end every 5 (5, 5, 4, 4) rows 15 (15, 17, 20, 20) times, working new sts into pattern, as possible—81 (81, 85, 91, 91) sts. Work to 19½ (20½, 20½, 21, 22)" from beg or desired length to shoulder. BO all sts evenly.

Finishing

Sew shoulder seams. With WS facing, size 9 needles, and MC, pick up 83 sts around neck edge. Knit back. Work in garter chevron patt, changing colors every 2 rows and following large stripe sequence from front. When 2" from neck edge, switch to size 10 needles and cont for 2" more. Switch to size 10½ needles and cont for 2". BO on next MC stripe. Set sleeves into armhole edge. Try on coat. Look at sleeve, and fold up extra length to create a cuff if desired. Pin in place. Sew side seams and sleeve seams, reversing sleeve seam at cuff fold. Tack sleeve to retain fold. With size H crochet hook and Dune, work 2 rows of sc along front bands, making buttonhole loops at neck edge on right front and then every 2" down front band for a total of 4 buttonhole loops. Fasten off. Sew buttons to left front.

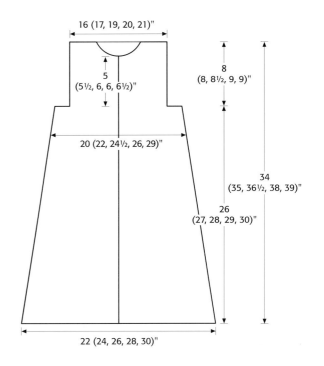

16 (17, 19, 20, 21)"

5 (5½, 6, 6, 6½)"

8 (8, 8½, 9, 9)"

20 (22, 24½, 26, 29)"

34 (35, 36½, 38, 39)"

26 (27, 28, 29, 30)"

22 (24, 26, 28, 30)"

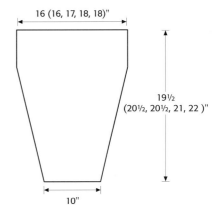

16 (16, 17, 18, 18)"

19½ (20½, 20½, 21, 22)"

10"

RAZZLE-DAZZLE

DESIGNED BY LAURA BRYANT

Neon green, sparkles and shine, big cables, lots of texture, and generous swing shaping—these are a few of my favorite things! They all come together in one great coat. It seems like a lot of elements, but the secret is to keep it simple: Instead of stripes or a tricky pattern stitch, the yarns are held together for a more subtle change of texture. Instead of allover cables, two big ones run up the fronts. Easy lapels that can be turned back or not require no neckline shaping at all, and a great garter stitch with contrasting I-cord edging frames the whole picture.

Style:	Coat
Length:	Long
Taper:	Wide hem to narrower bust
Sleeves:	Long, with modified-drop armhole shaping
Neckline:	Boat neck with slightly extended lapel edge

Finished Bust Measurement:

40 (44, 48, 52, 56)"

How Do I Vary from the Template?

✦ Taper is worked in four places: at side edges and in body, so taper is increased to 12 stitches and rate of taper is reduced.

✦ Adjustments are made for lapel.

✦ Sleeve is slightly larger and armhole deeper to accommodate under-garments.

✦ Adjustments are made for cables

✦ Sleeves are knit ½" shorter to allow for added border.

Materials

✦ 12 (13, 15, 16, 16) skeins Trendsetter Zucca (1.75oz, 77yds/skein), color 5135

✦ 7 (8, 9, 10, 10) skeins Prism Dazzle (1oz, 116yds/skein), color Chartreuse

✦ 2 (2½, 3, 3½, 3½) skeins Prism Light Stuff (6–8 oz, 400yds/skein), color Jelly Bean

✦ Trim only: 2 skeins Trendsetter Dolcino (1.75oz, 99yds/skein), color 61

✦ Size 11 needles

✦ Size 13 needles (or size required to obtain gauge)

✦ 5 large buttons

Gauge

2 stitches and 2½ rows = 1" in stockinette stitch on size 13 needles with all 3 yarns held together

Back

WITH SIZE 11 needles and all 3 yarns held together, CO 50 (54, 58, 64, 68) sts. Work 4 rows garter st, switch to size 13 needles, and place markers for shaping: K16 (18, 20, 23, 25), place marker, K18, place marker, K16 (18, 20, 23, 25). Work in St st to 8" from beg. Work dec row: K1, SSK, work to first marker, slip marker, SSK, work to within 2 sts of next marker, K2tog before marker, work to last 3 sts, K2tog, end K1—46 (50, 54, 60, 64) sts. Work to 15", rep dec row—42 (46, 50, 56, 60) sts rem. Work to 22", rep dec row—38 (42, 46, 52, 56) sts rem. Work to 30 (30, 31, 32, 34)" from beg or desired length to underarm. Shape armholes: BO 4 (5, 5, 6, 7) sts at beg of next 2 rows until 30 (32, 36, 40, 42) sts rem. Cont in St st until back is 40 (41, 42, 43, 45)" from beg. BO rem sts.

Fronts

WITH SIZE 11 needles and 3 yarns held together, CO 30 (32, 34, 36, 38) sts. Work 4 rows garter st, switch to size 13 needles, place marker for shaping, and work cable: K12 (13, 14, 15, 16), place marker, P2, K8, P2, K6 (7, 8, 9, 10). Working sts as set (knit the K sts and purl the P sts), on RS rows, work a cable crossing on 7th row and every 14th row thereafter: work to marker, P2 sts, sl next 4 sts to cn and hold in front, K4, K4 sts from cn, P2, finish row. At same time, at 8", work dec row: K1, SSK, work to within 2 sts of marker, K2tog, work across. Cont, working cable every 14 rows and working dec at 15" and 22". When piece is same length as back to armhole, shape armhole: BO 4 (5, 5, 6, 7) sts, cont on rem sts as established. When piece is same length as back, BO sts, knitting ctr 2 sts of cable tog, to last 10 sts. Place those 10 sts on holder. Work other front, reversing shaping.

Sleeves

WITH SIZE 11 needles and 3 yarns held together, CO 16 (17, 17, 18, 18) sts. Work garter st as for body. Switch to size 13 needles and work in St st, inc 1 st at each edge every 4 rows 14 (14, 15, 16, 16) times—44 (45, 47, 50, 50) sts. Work to 16 (16½, 17, 17½, 18)" from beg or desired length to underarm (measured upright to allow for downward stretch). Shape cap: BO 3 sts at beg of next 10 rows. BO rem sts.

Finishing

WITH SIZE 11 needles and 2 strands of Dolcino, pick up 16 (17, 17, 18, 18) sts along bottom of sleeve edge. Purl 1 row. CO 3 sts and work applied I-cord: *K2, SSK with last I-cord st and first st at sleeve bottom. Slide the 3 sts back to left needle, pull yarn tightly around back, and repeat from *. When 1 st remains on original band, BO sts as you work last row. Rep for other sleeve.

Sew shoulders together, working across cable and stopping at sts on holder. Set sleeves into armhole edge, between bound-off sts of armhole shaping. Sew side and sleeve seams, tacking side of sleeve to bound-off sts of armhole.

With size 11 needles and 3 yarns from body, pick up 62 (65, 67, 68, 70) sts up right front, place marker, pick up 10 sts from holder, 14 (15, 15, 16, 16) sts across back neck, 10 sts from holder, place marker, and pick up 62 (65, 67, 68, 70) sts down left front. Work 4 rows garter st, inc 1 st at each side of marker EOR (end at beg of WS row). Switch to size 13 needles and 2 strands Dolcino. Purl 1 row. Work attached I-cord as for sleeves, but to compensate for tighter gauge of Dolcino, every 3rd or 4th stitch, work 1 row of I-cord without attaching (omitting SSK). At same time, work 5 buttonholes on right front: work to first buttonhole, work 3 to 4 rows of I-cord unattached (omitting SSK), or desired width of button, BO 1 or 2 sts on band (or desired width of button, BO by slipping to right needle without knitting, then passing slipped sts over), reattaching I-cord after desired width, and at same time, work 2 rows of I-cord without attaching at neck corners. Sew buttons to left front.

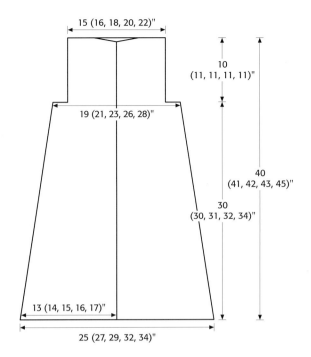

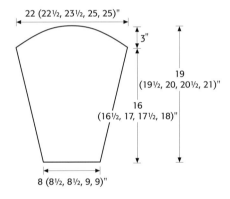

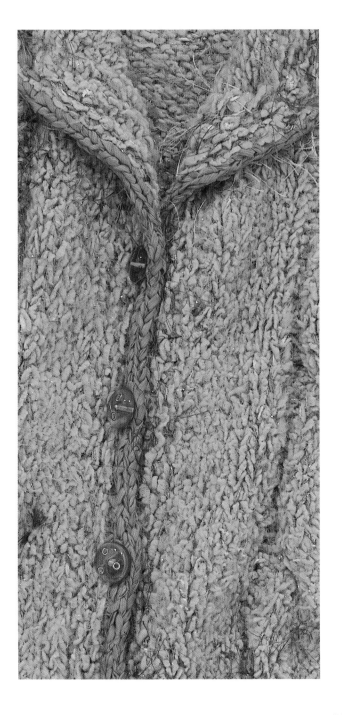

SWING ON A STAR

DESIGNED BY LAURA BRYANT

A glorious confection of sparkle, texture, and color zigzags its way into our hearts. One-row stripes mix up the colors and textures: the solid blue provides a frame, and the nubby texture of Cleo keeps the glitzy Super Dazzle from becoming overwhelming. This vest really pushes the use of the templates to the limit. Adjustments are made to accommodate the stitch multiple and the swing shaping. Swing can be built into a chevron easily by changing the number of straight stitches between the increases and decreases. The actual method is described in the pattern. This technique would be equally at home in a long coat with sleeves.

Style: Sleeveless coat

Length: Long

Taper: Wider hem to narrower bust

Armhole: Modified drop

Neckline: Deep V neck

Finished Bust Measurement:
34 (40, 46, 52)"

How Do I Vary from the Template?

✦ Swing is built into the body of the garment by changing the number of stitches worked between the increases and decreases of the Chevron stitch. The taper is not worked at the side seams and at darts, but in separate actions where many decreases are made in one row, at several different points up the length.

✦ Armhole bind offs and neckline shaping are adjusted for the pattern repeat.

Materials

✦ (A) 8 (9, 10, 11) skeins Prism Trillino (2oz, 85yds/skein)

✦ (B) 5 (6, 7, 9) skeins Prism Cleo (1.5oz, 82yds/skein)

✦ (C) 5 (6, 7, 8) skeins Prism Super Dazzle (1oz, 90yds/skein)

✦ Size 8 needles (or size required to obtain gauge)

✦ Size 11 needles

✦ Size F crochet hook

✦ 1 large button

Colors on model: Trillino 499, Cleo Nevada, Super Dazzle Tumbleweed; alternate colorway: Trillino 638, Cleo Ginger, Super Dazzle Fog

Gauge

2 repeats (27 sts) = 5½" and 18 rows = 4" in chevron stitch, working 1 row of each yarn, on size 8 needles

Chevron Stitch

(Multiple of 12 plus 3)

Row 1: K1, SSK, *K4, YO, K1, YO, K4, sl 2 tog as if to knit, K1, p2sso; rep from *, end K4, YO, K1, YO, K4, K2tog, K1.

Row 2: Purl.

Rep rows 1 and 2.

NOTES

✦ Swing is built into the body by having more stitches at the bottom third than the middle and fewer stitches at the top. Check your gauge according to the multiple above, which is for the middle section, then read the pattern for directions on the extra stitches at cast-on and the subsequent decreasing.

✦ The length of this garment causes the knitting to stretch substantially, and as it stretches, it also narrows. We have taken this into account, and to achieve both the correct girth and length measurement, the instructions show more stitches needed and a shorter length than the finish will be. The garment will grow in length approximately 5" and will narrow in girth approximately 6". Select your size from our stated finished measurements. If you were using the templates, you would need to select a size three sizes larger to achieve a correct fit.

✦ The repeat in this pattern is maintained by beginning and ending each row 1 with only half of a repeat for shaping: notice that the first decrease is an SSK instead of the sl 2, K1, p2sso of the repeat; and the row ends with a K2tog. Keep this in mind when you are decreasing for neck shaping. If each row started with the full repeat, you would be adding stitches every right-side row.

✦ The stripe sequence is one row of each color: Cast on with A, drop A, attach B, work across, drop B, attach C, work back, and A is waiting for you.

✦ When carrying the yarns up the edge, be careful not to pull the first stitch too tightly or the edges will pull up.

Back

WITH SIZE 11 needles and A, CO 143 (171, 199, 227) sts. Switch to size 8 needles and work 1 row of each yarn, establishing patt in garter st as follows:

Row 1: K1, SSK, *K5, YO, K1, YO, K5, sl 2 tog as if to knit, K1, p2sso; rep from *, end K5, YO, K1, YO, K5, K2tog, K1.

Row 2: Knit.

Rep last 2 rows 4 times.

Change row 2 to purl and work rows 1 and 2 to 13½ (14, 14½, 15)" from beg. Be sure to measure by holding up the piece to allow for downward stretch and measure to the points.

First swing decrease: Row 1: K1, sl 2, K2tog, p2sso, *K4, YO, K1, YO, K4, sl 3, K2tog, p3sso; rep from *, end K4, YO, K1, YO, K4, K3tog—123 (147, 171, 195) sts.

Row 2: Purl.

Beg Chevron st as written for gauge. Work even to 27 (28, 29, 30)" from beg, then work:

2nd swing decrease: K1, sl 2, K2tog, p2sso, *K3, YO, K1, YO, K3, sl 3, K2tog, p3sso; rep from *, end K3, YO, K1, YO, K3, K3tog— 103 (123, 143, 163) sts. From now on, work 3 sts instead of 4 between increases and decreases. Work to 31 (31, 32, 34)" from beg or desired length to underarm. Shape armholes: BO 12 sts at beg of next 2 rows—79 (99, 119, 139) sts. Work as established to 39 (40, 41, 43)" from beg. BO rem sts.

Fronts

WITH SIZE 11 needles and A, CO 73 (87, 101, 115) sts. Work as for back to armhole, then shape armhole at beg of row only. Work 1" more, then shape neck: dec 1 st at neck edge every other row 12 times. Note that in chevron st, the first and last repeats end with dec of only 1 st, whereas in patt repeats, it is 2 dec sts to offset the 2 inc sts. As you dec for neck edge, you must keep this same edging, so when 6 sts have been decreased, you will beg patt with an inc, and you must do only 1 (K1, YO). When all 12 sts have been decreased, you are back to patt as written above. When same length as back from beg, BO all sts. Make other front, reversing shaping.

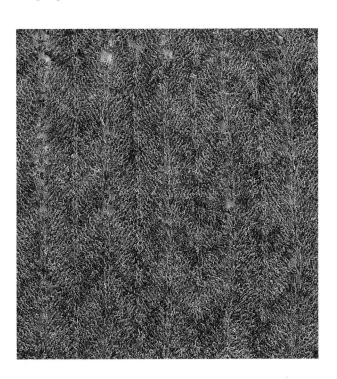

Finishing

WITH SIZE F crochet hook and A, work 3 rows of sc along each side edge, fronts, and back. Sew shoulder seams. Sew side seams from top to bottom for about 16 (17, 18, 19)", leaving a slit of 16" or desired opening. With A, work 3 rows sc around front and neck edges, working 2 sts at neck corner and working a button loop at the right neck corner on last row. Work 1 rnd rev sc around entire front, neck, bottom, and slit edges. Work 1 rnd sc and 1 rnd rev sc around armhole edges. Sew button to left front.

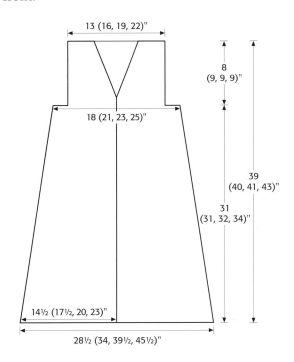

13 (16, 19, 22)"

8 (9, 9, 9)"

18 (21, 23, 25)"

39 (40, 41, 43)"

31 (31, 32, 34)"

14½ (17½, 20, 23)"

28½ (34, 39½, 45½)"

TRICKS OF THE TRADE FOR FABULOUS FINISHING

You've gathered up the ingredients and now you're ready to put the meal together. Finishing the sweater is like taking those ingredients and joining them into a feast to wear. Good finishing ensures that the sweater sits properly across your shoulders, the sleeve length is perfect, and the sweater fits around the body without pulling. All of your work up to this point should make putting the pieces together a piece of cake. If you selected the size that best fits your desired measurements and your gauge was right, the finished sweater will fit.

Blocking

We recommend blocking your stitch gauge before you block the knit pieces. It is better to test your swatch for any problems and go from there. Gently block through a damp towel placed over the wrong side of your knitting. This technique will keep any direct heat away from the sweater. In case of a problem, such as scorching your knitting, the damage will be on the wrong side and you will still be able to salvage your work.

Use T-pins to keep the pieces flat. Refer to the knitting diagram and measure as the pieces are pinned out, making sure you don't pull things out of shape. Blocking (depending on the materials you have used) can help make the pieces more to your desired size in case your gauge changed or your body changed. Remember that blocking pieces wider will make them shorter and blocking pieces longer will make them narrower. As you start to steam the pieces, pay careful attention to the edges. Clean, flat edges will allow you to find a perfect edge stitch and make a narrow seam. Do not put the weight of the iron directly onto the pieces. Once steamed, remove the damp towel and allow the work to dry. Remove all pins and remeasure the pieces to be sure that everything became the size you needed.

Putting It All Together

Shoulder Seams

We recommend that you start with the shoulder seams. Since the shoulder area carries the weight of the entire sweater, special attention should be paid to ensure that the pieces are tightly joined and will hold. Many people enjoy knitting their shoulder seams together. While this technique works, it is not something we recommend. A shoulder that is knit together will have a narrow seam, yet the weight of all of the pieces can stretch the seam, often causing the sleeves to become too long and the sleeve cap attachment to sag down the arm. In addition, the most common area to break open is the shoulder seam. If this happens with a shoulder seam that has been knit together, live (open) stitches can run. We recommend binding off all shoulder edges and then joining them together firmly.

To weave shoulder seams:

Our shoulder weaving technique is also known as *invisible, blind, mattress,* or *Kitchener* stitch. To work, place two pieces right sides up on a table,

with the edges to be seamed adjacent. With a threaded tapestry needle, insert the needle into the V of the first stitch on the piece nearest you, then into the V of the first stitch on the other piece. Insert the needle through both threads that make the V of the next stitch on the piece nearest you, then through the same V of the other piece. Pull the tension just enough so the stitch you have made looks like the knitting. Repeat across, then fasten off and weave in the end.

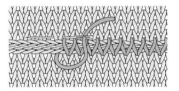

This provides an almost invisible seam, but it may need to be reinforced with a slip stitch on the inside. If you've used heavy yarns, especially if the garment is a coat or jacket, you may need to hand or machine stitch a piece of twill tape along the shoulder line and across the back neck to stabilize the knitting.

To slip stitch shoulder seams:

Another alternative is to slip stitch pieces together. This technique is worked with a crochet hook and will create the firmest seam possible of any of the finishing techniques.

1. With right sides facing and starting at the side edge, insert a crochet hook through the same stitch on each piece and pull up a loop.

2. Insert the hook through the next stitch of both pieces and pull up another loop. Pull the new loop through the first loop on the hook to slip them together. One loop remains.

3. Go into the next stitch of both pieces and repeat the slip-stitch process across the row. As you work, pull the work tightly as needed to add stability to the seam, or leave loose.

4. When finished, cut the yarn and pull the strand through the remaining loop to fasten off.

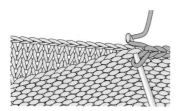

One benefit to slip-stitch seaming is that the work can be turned over easily to see the pieces as they come together. If you need to fix anything, it rips easily and goes back together faster the second time. Practice different techniques on some of your swatches until you are comfortable with them all. No matter which finishing technique you use, always bury the tail and secure it.

Once the shoulder seams are joined, join the sleeves to the body by centering the sleeve cap to the shoulder seam and pinning it in place. Attach the yarn and seam the sleeve cap into place along the armhole edge either by the "in and out" (see side seams below) or slip-stitch method. Once the sleeve cap is in place, try on the sweater. Check how the shoulders fit and be sure that the sleeve cap is even. The weight of the sweater will cause the neckline to pull. We suggest that you put together the balance of the side seams and underarm seams next. Work from the bottom of each piece up toward the underarm.

Side Seams

We prefer seaming vertical seams with a woven stitch that is worked from the right side of your knitting and weaves your seams together invisibly. This technique works like a zipper and pulls the knit pieces together as they are joined. Some knitters prefer to add two stitches to a pattern so that no pattern repeats will be lost and the sweater will not become narrower. You must have clean edges and stay in the same row for the entire seam. When knitting, consider working shaping in "full fashion"

(see page 143), increasing or decreasing as directed in the pattern, one or two stitches in from the edge at all times, to produce a clean edge for seaming. Full-fashion shaping will also add detail and give the finished sweater a more professional look.

The weaving stitch is worked from the right side of the knitting. Place the pieces on a flat surface with right sides up and aligned along the edges to be brought together. Begin at the lower edge, either with the long tail from your cast-on or with a new piece of yarn attached firmly on the wrong side of the work and brought to the right side. If the yarn from the sweater is textured, select a different yarn with a smooth texture for seaming, matching the color as closely as possible.

Insert the needle under two horizontal bars between the first and second stitches from the edge, then under two stitches at the same place on the opposite piece. Pull the yarn firmly in the direction of the seam. Be sure to go into the stitch you came out of and then proceed up, working under two horizontal bars on each side and pulling it together as you work. The most common mistake is when you don't "go in where you came out." I like to think of it as a song, "In where I came out and up two." If you sing it as you work, the seam will come together beautifully.

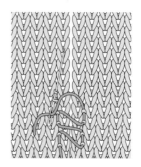

Bands and Borders

ONCE THE sweater is put together, you must decide on bands, borders, necklines, and trims. In most cases, bottom-edge and sleeve-edge borders will be worked as you knit the pieces. A bit more planning is required for front bands. While ribbing at the bottom, cuffs, and necklines should have some elasticity to pull in a bit, ribbing that is picked up along a front band and knit toward the center should be gauged to sit just right. Garter stitch or pinstriped bands are even more critical because the knitted patterns themselves have little give. Fortunately, there are some easy steps to take that will ensure perfectly finished fronts.

Since the front bands will be one of the last steps in completing your garment, you can use a gauge you've already made: the band at the bottom of the sweater. Hold the back up sideways, so the border is in the same direction as it will sit on the front, and while a friend holds the piece this way, take a total measurement of the border from one edge to the other. This mimics how the garment will behave when the same border is on the front. Divide the measurement by the number of stitches in the band, and you have a border gauge. Measure along the front edge of the sweater and multiply this measurement by the border gauge, and you have the number of stitches to pick up along the front. The same can be done around the neck edge, with the garment lying flat and a flexible tape measure going around the curves. For a V neck, measure from the bottom to the beginning of the neck, then again along the neck to the shoulder, and finally across the back neck. Keep the number of stitches to each point separate, to help in picking them up evenly and centered.

With the right side of the left front facing, and using the same needle that you used for the other borders, pick up and knit the required number of stitches evenly spaced along the body edge. Work in the border pattern for the desired width and bind off in pattern. Make sure that your bind-off is neither too tight (band will pull up) nor too loose (band will waver and not lie flat.) Measure the left band for the button spacing, keeping in mind that if it is a crew neck, you will also put a buttonhole

in the neckband. Make the right band, making buttonholes that correspond to the button spacing in the middle of the width.

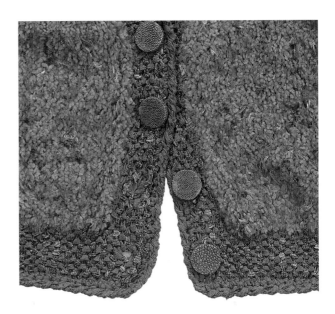

Attached border

If picking up stitches scares you, another answer to borders is to work them separately and attach them. The advantage to this is that you don't have to pick up any stitches and there is no guessing involved. Figure out the width of the band and multiply this by your band gauge. Cast on these stitches and work in pattern until the band is ½" smaller than the front edge from the bottom to the neck shaping. Put the stitches on a holder. Weave the band in place along the front edge, working from the bottom up. Pick up the stitches from the holder and add extra rows, if necessary, or rip out rows if too many were worked. Bind off the remaining stitches and finish adding the band. If you truly plan ahead, you can incorporate your band stitches into the number of stitches from your front bottom border stitches and work them together up to the body. Once the bottom band is finished, place the front-band stitches onto a stitch holder and save them for later while you work the body. Don't forget to put a buttonhole in the center of the right front band when working the bottom border.

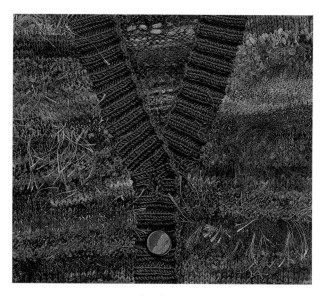

Neck-edge miter

When picking up stitches for a V-neck cardigan, you can do a continuous band that miters at the beginning of the neck shaping. When picking up, work to within one stitch of the beginning of the neck shaping, place a marker, pick up the next two stitches, place a marker, then pick up the remaining stitches to the shoulder and across the back neck; repeat marker placement down the other side. When working the bands, increase on each side of the two markers every fourth row, working the new stitches into the pattern where possible.

Mitered corner at V

Working border bands separately for a V neck is also an option. Work as for a crew neck and continue until the band is long enough to reach the center of the back neck. While this method is effective, it does not take into consideration the V-neck shape and will soften the edge, whereas the pick-up method highlights the detail of a crisper corner.

For a crew-neck cardigan, you can do a continuous garter band that miters at the neck corners: pick up the front-band stitches up to the neck shaping, place marker, pick up neck stitches around, placing a marker at the opposite front corner; pick up down the other front, then increase at each side of each marker every other row. The rate of increase is greater because the corner is sharper and the pattern is garter stitch, which has more rows per inch than stockinette or rib stitch.

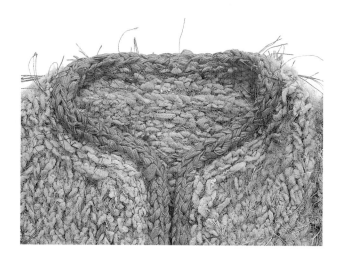

Mitered corner at neck top and applied I-cord

To finish the neck edge of an attached border band, work the front as written on page 139 and, instead of binding off the stitches when you reach the neck shaping, leave them on a holder. Once both bands are attached, start at the front edge of the right front. Work across the front stitch holders in pattern. Pick up the stitches around the neck edge with the number of stitches needed to fit the pattern multiple. Continue across the final front holder. Work in the border pattern for the desired length and bind off in pattern.

Applied I-cord that is attached as a final edge to a garter band is a great look. I-cord is tubular knitting that is knit every row without turning on a double-pointed needle (the stitches are slid back to the other end of the needle, and the yarn is pulled tightly from behind to begin the new row). When worked in this manner, a tube of stockinette can be used in many decorative ways. This same cord can be simultaneously knit and attached to an edge with a few simple steps.

First, decide how large the finished cord will be. It can be as small as two stitches, which makes a slightly corded edge that looks like a chain, or as large as five or six stitches if you wish a truly tubular edge. Of course, the gauge of the yarn will also guide you. Very thick yarn will work for a tube with only two or three stitches, while a thin yarn may need more to look important.

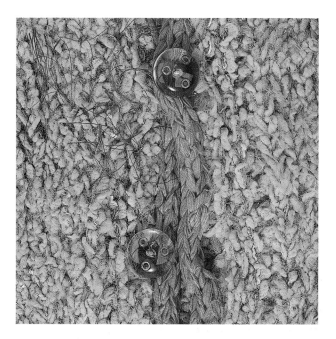

Attached I-cord and buttonhole

Work a garter stitch band on the finished body pieces by picking up stitches. Keep the garter stitches on the needles. Don't bind off. At the beginning of the next right-side row, cast on the desired number of I-cord stitches using the cable cast-on method. Knit all but the last cast-on stitch, then SSK the last stitch with the first stitch of the border. Slide the stitches back to the left needle, pull the yarn tightly to the beginning of the row and work across to the last I-cord stitch, then SSK the last stitch with the first border stitch. Continue until all border stitches are used. On the last row, bind off each stitch as you work across.

If you wish to make a buttonhole, work the I-cord without the SSK for two or three rows (the desired width of the buttonhole), then bind off the corresponding stitches on the band (without carrying the yarn: slip two stitches to the right-hand needle, pass first stitch over second, and repeat as necessary), then resume the SSK to join. This look is very tailored and really finishes an edge.

Another alternative to knitting borders is crochet. There is no formula for crochet edges because crochet and knit gauges differ. Use a crochet border stitch that will finish the edges nicely and help them lie flat. Some simple crochet border stitches are:

+ *Slip Stitch:* Insert hook into stitch, wrap yarn around hook and pull loop through stitch, then pull loop through stitch on the hook. Repeat around. This type of edge keeps things flat and does not build width. It is a simple edge that evens things out.

+ *Single Crochet (sc):* Insert hook into stitch, wrap yarn around hook and pull loop through stitch, wrap yarn around hook and pull loop through both stitches on hook. Repeat around. This will also finish off an edge but adds thickness and will build rows.

✦ *Reverse Single Crochet (rev sc):* Worked like single crochet but in reverse from left to right along the edge row. Also known as *crab stitch* or *rope crochet* and not always easy to do. It is best to have a row of slip stitch or single crochet established first and then work the reverse single crochet.

Reverse single crochet on a foundation row
of single crochet

There are many additional crochet borders that create picot edges or lace borders, and a good crochet book provides many options. Keep in mind that crochet borders are usually decorative.

Crocheted edging

Whether picking up, sewing on, or crocheting your borders, once everything is done, you are ready to go out and be a fashion model. You started with a simple skein of yarn and made a gauge. You took body measurements and found your numbers on a template spreadsheet. You transferred your numbers onto a knitting diagram and off you went, watching your measurements and checking your gauge as your work progressed. Now the pieces are finished and you have successfully put it all together. The finishing touches are complete and you are successful. Try the sweater on and smile. We make a great team. Enjoy!

GLOSSARY AND ABBREVIATIONS

approx	approximately
beg	begin(ning)
CC	contrast color
ch	chain
cn	cable needle
CO	cast on
cont	continue
ctr	center
dec	decrease, decreasing
EOR	every other row
full-fashion decrease	on knit side: K1, SSK, work to last 3 sts; K2tog, K1. On purl side: P1, sl 1 as if to knit, P1, psso, work to last 3 sts; P2tog, P1. This places the dec inside of the edge stitch. Sometimes worked with 2 or 3 sts at edge.
garter stitch	knit every row
inc	increase, increasing
K	knit
Kitchener stitch	a method of weaving seams invisibly (see page 00)
MC	main color
psso	pass slipped stitch over
p2sso	pass 2 slipped stitches over
p3sso	pass 3 slipped stitches over
patt	pattern
ply	an individual strand of thread within a thicker strand of yarn
P	purl
rem	remain(ing)

rep	repeat
rev sc	reverse single crochet
rev St st	reverse stockinette stitch: purl RS rows, knit WS rows
rib	combination of knits and purls that line up row after row: for example, K1, P1 every row; can be done in any multiples (K2, P2, etc.)
rnd	round
RS	right side
sl st	slip stitch from left to right needle as if to purl unless specified otherwise
sl 1, K1, psso	slip 1 as if to knit, knit 1, pass slipped stitch over knit stitch
sc	single crochet
SSK	slip, slip, knit: slip as if to knit, slip as if to knit, insert left needle into front of the 2 stitches, knit the 2 stitches together. May replace slip 1, K1, psso (see above) for smoother shaping.
st(s)	stitch(es)
St st	stockinette stitch; knit RS rows, purl WS rows
wyib	with yarn in back
wyif	with yarn in front
WS	wrong side
YO	yarn over the needle from front to back

RESOURCES

FOR A LIST of shops in your area or mail-order/Internet companies that carry the yarns and buttons mentioned in this book, write to the following companies:

FRONT AND CENTER BUTTONS
16745 Saticoy St., #101
Van Nuys, CA 91406

GREAT YARNS
4023 Rucker Ave.
Everett, WA 98201
Rhinestone zippers

MUENCH YARNS
285 Bel Marin Keys Blvd.
Novato, CA 94949

PRISM
2595 30th Avenue North
St. Petersburg, FL 33713

TRENDSETTER YARNS AND LANE BORGOSESIA
16745 Saticoy St., #101
Van Nuys, CA 91406

BIBLIOGRAPHY

Stanfield, Lesley. *The New Knitting Stitch Library.* Asheville, N.C.: Lark Books, 1998.

Walker, Barbara G. *A Treasury of Knitting Patterns.* Pittsville, Wis.: Schoolhouse Press, 1998.

Walker, Barbara G. *A Second Treasury of Knitting Patterns.* Pittsville, Wis.: Schoolhouse Press, 1998.